ADVANCE PRAISE FOR

WELL AT WORK

At a time when so many of us are not well at work, Jessica Grossmeier shines a light on how we can each reclaim meaning, connection, and a sense of humanity in our daily work life. **Well At Work** is an indispensable guide to thriving in the midst of today's challenging workplace.

Laura Putnam, MA
Author of *Workplace Wellness that Works*
Cofounder, Upli

What a resource! **Well At Work** is an inspiring, comprehensive, practical guide that will promote thriving in your work and life.

Jack Bastable
President, Vital Leadership

Well At Work is the must-read practice guide to investigate the intimate and vulnerable place where your well-being rests, waiting to be awoken. The activities and stories illuminate pathways to connect to your own values, meaning, and purpose to live a life of fulfillment and connection.

Derek Bell, MS
VP Solutions & Clinical Operations, VITAL WorkLife
Educator, University of Wisconsin–Stevens Point
Host, Highway to Well podcast

Well At Work is required curriculum for lifelong learners. Inspiring storytelling takes you on a self-discovery journey, with practical steps to chart the best path forward to more fulfilling work and thriving in life.

Kathy Meacham Webb, MBA
Owner, Kathy Webb Consulting

Life is change; growth is optional. Whether you are feeling challenged navigating an ever-changing world or finding yourself in a job that no longer has the same energetic zing to it, **Well At Work** is the guide you need. This book offers thoughtful opportunities for reflection and practical guidance to enable you to choose growth that aligns with your authentic purpose and values.

Susan Morgan Bailey, MS, SPHR, SHRM-SCP
Workplace Culture Consultant
Founder, Rooted Soul Coaching

Well At Work is more than a book — it's a trusted companion for anyone seeking greater meaning, connection, and well-being in their work and life. Jessica Grossmeier masterfully blends honest stories, research-based insights, and practical exercises into an inspiring journey of self-discovery and empowerment. Whether you're navigating uncertainty or striving for greater alignment, **Well At Work** will meet you where you are and guide you toward a more fulfilling, enlivened way of being.

Patty Purpur de Vries, MS
Author, *Living Well Within*
Chief Experience Officer, Living Well USA

Well-being is a journey, not a destination. **Well At Work** is a personal guide to reframe perspective, find balance and embrace one's full potential. A must read for anyone seeking greater purpose and alignment in their work!

Lexie Dendrinelis
Owner, Living Well Leadership

WELL AT WORK

Chart Your Course with Purpose, Connection, and Transcendence

JESSICA GROSSMEIER, PHD, MPH
with Rhea Fix, MEd, SPHR

Jessica Grossmeier Consulting
Morgan Hill, CA USA
www.jessicagrossmeier.com

Published 2025

Cover design and interior artwork: Keely Rochelle Fix Goss

Author photo courtesy of Christopher J. Grossmeier

ISBN: 979-8-218-70843-6 (paperback)

DISCLAIMER

Neither the author nor the publisher assumes any responsibility for errors, omissions, or contrary interpretations of the subject matter within.

To Dr. Paul Terry, for many years of collaboration, mentorship, and friendship.
It's a potent and powerful gift that's fueled my well-being at work.

AND

In memory of Dr. Sheryl Niebuhr,
for sharing her early vision of well-being at work
and encouraging me to dream bigger.

Contents

PART ONE

Get Your Bearings

Well At Work

Chapter 1
Wake-Up Call

"In the absence of wake-up calls, many of us
never really confront the critical issues of life."

Stephen Covey, author, educator, businessman, speaker

My Wake-Up Call

I lay on the cold wooden floor, eyes closed, wondering what's happened. Aren't I supposed to be flying somewhere today? Did I fall asleep during yoga meditation again? No, something is definitely wrong. An unfamiliar throb of pain is radiating from the side of my face. Pain aside, it feels good to be still and lying down. My mind begins to drift and then suddenly I notice that someone is talking. It's my husband, Chris. I keep my eyes closed and strain to focus on what he's saying.

"I'm not sure what happened. I heard a loud sound like something falling on the floor. I thought maybe one of our cats knocked something over. I got up and went into the living room and found my wife lying face down on the floor. I turned her over onto her back and she coughed up blood. She isn't responding to me, and I think she might be unconscious."

Wait a minute. I fell? I wasn't breathing? I'm unconscious? I coughed up blood?! Maybe I've finally done it. I've pushed myself too hard and I've injured myself. The thought jars me awake and I flicker my eyes open to see Chris crouched over me with his phone in his hand. He's giving someone our street address. Then he sees my eyes open and calls out to me, "Jess! Can you hear me? If you can, don't move, just blink your eyes a couple of times."

I blink my eyes to let him know that I hear him, and he exclaims into the phone, "She's conscious! She just opened her eyes and blinked a couple of times when I asked her to."

He looks into my eyes and says, "Don't move, you fell. I'm talking to 911."

Then he directs his attention back to his conversation on the phone, appearing to be listening to instructions. I close my eyes, take a few deep breaths through my nose, and try to make sense out of my circumstances. The last thing I remember was that I was about to get into the shower and that I felt dizzy. I lay back down in bed for a moment, trying to figure out what to do. I had a plane to catch for a business trip and if I lay in bed too long, I would miss my flight. I decided to get up and eat something. Then, nothing. What happened?

Chris wraps up the call with the paramedics, and he's as curious as I am.

He asks me, "Do you have any idea why you fell? Did you trip over the cat or something?" I tell him that I was dizzy when I got up to shower and decided to get a banana and lay down on the sofa. Apparently, I never made it to the kitchen. It's a story I repeat several times over the course of the day as I make my way through a labyrinth of visits with health-care professionals from the admitting nurse at the emergency room, to the ER physician who gives me stitches, to the X-ray technician and finally to the resident specialist who confirms I broke my jaw by the fall. I feel a flood of emotions: guilty about missing the business trip; disappointed that I wouldn't be able to present my dissertation research at the professional conference; ashamed about not keeping up the pace at work; relief about having a good reason to rest. I've been so bone-crushingly tired these past few months and have longed for a break. But a broken jaw was not the kind of break I'd been longing for.

I am consoled when the specialist recommends that I not have surgery to get my jaw wired shut. She suggests that because I only broke the jaw in one place, the bone could mend on its own without having to immobilize it artificially. That is, if I avoid anything that could disrupt the alignment of the jaw. This means no running, no chewing of any kind, no extended time talking, and giving up caffeine because it interferes with bone growth. I nod as I take in her instructions, overwhelmed by the implications of this injury on my work and life in general.

In between care visits, Chris calls the airline to let them know I missed my flight due to a medical emergency and cancels my hotel reservations and the car that was supposed to pick me up from the airport. He lets my boss know what happened and says we'll be in touch with updates once we know more. My boss arranges for another colleague to cover the presentation I was to give at the conference and asks us to let her know when I'll be back at work.

Over the next week, I get in touch with my primary care physician, and he orders a full workup to determine if an underlying heart issue is what led me to faint. I am relieved when he tells me that everything looks fine, and my fainting spell is likely due to extreme dehydration and exhaustion. He orders me to slow down and rest. I am relieved that there is not something more serious going on with my health and think maybe this is the wake-up call I've needed to realign my priorities.

What Is Your Wake-Up Call?

My wake-up call moment was somewhat dramatic, but sometimes we get signals from within us or through the people in our lives that something might need to change. Not everyone experiences this call for a major life adjustment in response to a single life event. For some, these questions surface over a period of months or years.

Self-Reflection: Why Are You Here?

What drew you to pick up this guide or what do you hope to learn from it?

....

....

....

What are the signs and signals in your life that indicate something may need to change? How do you know when something in your life might need to change or be adjusted in some way?

....

....

....

Have you experienced a wake-up call in your own life? If so, how did that unfold for you—dramatically or more subtly?

....

....

....

What's True for You?

As you reflect on your life, are any of the following statements true for you?

Check all that apply and add any statements that represent how you feel right now.

- ☐ I sometimes wonder if I am focusing on the right priorities in my life.
- ☐ I take on more than I should and have a hard time saying "no" to new opportunities.
- ☐ I sometimes wonder if people only care about what I can do for them, but don't really care about me as a person.
- ☐ I am eager to feel stronger connections at work, but I'm not sure how to get past surface-level conversations.
- ☐ I want to spend time with people who matter to me but find myself withdrawing from social activities because I don't have the energy to socialize.
- ☐ I take time to have fun, but it's temporary and I long for a deeper, more enduring sense of joy.
- ☐ I cannot identify the last time I felt truly happy or at peace.
- ☐ Most days, I wake up with a sense of dread or overwhelmed with all that I must do.
- ☐ I used to enjoy my work, but lately I find myself wondering why I am working so hard.
- ☐ When I take time off from work, I feel guilty, even though I've earned the time off.
- ☐ I can name many things I appreciate about my job, so I feel confused when feelings of dissatisfaction with my job surface.
- ☐ I like my job, but I wonder if it is possible to feel more fulfilled by it.
- ☐ I can point to a lot of things that I'm grateful for in my life and don't understand why feelings of discontent sometimes surface.
- ☐ Other statements:

Who Should Read This Book

This book is for anyone who has wondered if it's possible to feel more connected, aligned, and fulfilled in their work and in their life. If several of the statements above resonate, this book is written for you. If none of these thoughts have surfaced for you, this book may still be helpful to explore how to align your work with your personal well-being goals.

This chapter is about wake-up calls. Big or small, we've all had times in our life when we've wondered how things could be different than they are. It's common for "what if" questions to emerge when something is out of alignment in your life.

> *A sense of inner restlessness and discomfort is hard-wired into us for a reason. It's intended to draw our attention, to invite tapping into a deeper well of inner wisdom.*

There is no reason to feel ashamed or guilty if these questions are surfacing in you. You are not alone. Most of us want more in life than to simply get along with others and get by.

This book is about the role that our work (or responsibilities that consume a significant chunk of our waking hours) may play in our sense of well-being. There are millions of people just like you who seek a satisfying work experience that doesn't leave them feeling too depleted to pursue what matters most to them in life. Research shows most people expect to experience joy and fulfillment in their work. In this moment, you might be wondering if that's even possible.

When Well-Being Practices Don't Lead to Thriving

One of the things I learned from my wake-up call moment was that my own well-being practices were not fully addressing what I needed to thrive in my personal and work life.

While I didn't know it at the time, my experiences with exhaustion, burnout, and disengagement with work are not unique to me. These are systemic issues emerging at epidemic levels in workplaces across the globe. My first book, *Reimagining Workplace Well-Being,* was written to support organizations, business leaders, and anyone leading employee well-being efforts in their organizations to build a workplace environment that addresses threats to employee well-being. A few leading organizations have risen to the challenge of redesigning policies, working environments, and ways of working to support employee well-being. However, it's hard work and most organizations are still figuring out how to adjust traditional business and leadership practices to address burnout, loneliness, and employee disengagement in their work.

As I write this guide in 2025, it seems like some organizations are headed in the opposite direction from the strategies recommended in my 2022 book. Some organizations continue to emphasize organizational profitability and performance at the expense of the well-being of their workers. This trend suggests that organizations lack understanding of the benefits of investing in workforce well-being, including increased employee engagement with their work, higher levels of performance, and financial organizational success.

How This Guide Is Structured

If you find the ideas in this guide compelling and want to try to influence your organization to think about policies, practices, and resources that better support the well-being of workers, *Reimagining Workplace Well-Being* offers some guidance. But you don't need to read my original book to fully benefit from this guide, which is written for individuals like you.

The good news is, there are many ways we can prioritize our own well-being. This guide is for anyone who wants to take proactive steps to find more meaning and fulfillment in their work and in their life *right* now. This is not necessarily about changing your job, but rather about imagining new ways of working that align your work with what matters most to you, allowing you show up in the world as the best version of yourself. If you are considering a job change, the exercises in this guide may help you clarify what kinds of working conditions will support your well-being.

Applying This Guide to Your Journey

As someone who has journeyed through the valley of exhaustion, burnout, disconnection, and disengagement from a job that I once loved, I am familiar with the process of navigating back to a place of personal and professional thriving. Over the past 15 years, I've dug into decades of research and thousands of years of wisdom practices to identify the waypoints and steppingstones towards a more meaningful, connected, and fulfilling life. Knowing how helpful these practices have been for my well-being, this guide aims to translate research into everyday actions that can support you in your well-being.

Throughout this guide, I'll share the steps that I took to identify, establish, and maintain the well-being practices that help me to show up as the best version of myself no matter what work or responsibilities I'm focused on (*my well-being story*). I share *my well-being story* to inspire your thinking about the best path forward for *your well-being story*. Through self-reflections and practical exercises, you'll **Chart Your Course** towards more satisfying, aligned, and fulfilling work.

> Your **Well-Being Story** reflects the steps you take to identify, establish, and maintain practices that help you show up as the best version of yourself.

Part One of this guide invites you to consider what it *means to you* to live your best life and reflect on the influence of your work on your well-being. I'll share research that affirms why we need to develop new ways of working that better support whole person well-being – and how current working practices may fall short for many of us.

Chapter 2 guides you in defining what it means for you to *pursue* your own well-being. Even though workplace well-being has been the focus for my work for more than 30 years, I cannot determine what it looks like and feels like for you to be living life to its fullest. Well-being is personal and only you can identify the dimensions that you feel called to address right now.

Chapter 3 introduces the spiritual dimension of well-being as one area to consider as part of whole person well-being. I recognize that this term "spiritual" comes with some baggage and it might not feel like something you want to address. It's okay to approach the chapter with some skepticism or critique. I understand the resistance to this topic because I was once discouraged from pursuing this dimension of well-being as part of my work. I heeded that caution for a while, but there is growing consensus that spirituality is part of an evidence-based approach to whole person well-being. It's helpful to be able to distinguish how spirituality differs from religion. I'll share more about definitions in chapter 3 and you'll be invited to consider what resonates for you.

My approach to spiritual well-being focuses on three broad areas of research: purpose (connection to self), social connection (connection to others), and transcendence (connection to something bigger than yourself). If anything in this guide feels uncomfortable, pay attention to the discomfort and ask yourself where it might be coming from. Feel free to skip a section or an exercise and move on to other areas. You can always come back to it later if you choose to do so.

The final chapter in Part One (**chapter 4**) considers the role of work for our well-being. Whether work represents a full-time or part-time paid position or unpaid work that you do as a student, caregiver, or volunteer, how we spend the majority of our waking hours has a substantial impact on our well-being. It could be largely positive and supportive or a significant challenge to our well-being. In most cases, it's a mixture of both and we'll explore the influence you have on how work supports or diminishes your well-being.

Chapters in **Part Two** of this guide focus on science-backed strategies and practices that can make work feel more meaningful and supportive of our well-being, including deepening our sense of purpose in life, our connections with other people, and our connection with something bigger than ourselves, which I call transcendence.

Chapters 5 through 7 address each of these three areas:

Purpose - a strong sense of direction for one's life; an overarching aspiration that energizes one's efforts and provides a central source of meaning and significance.

Social connection – being in relationship with others who leave you feeling seen, heard, and valued, providing a sense of support and belonging.

Transcendence - to rise above or go beyond our ordinary limits or everyday experience; connecting with something bigger than yourself.

Each chapter in Part Two follows the pattern you'll notice in Part One of the guide: my well-being story, self-reflection prompts that invite you to consider your well-being story, and some science-backed principles that support the ideas in the chapter. Part Two introduces specific practices that will help you develop new skills or approaches to supporting your well-being at and through your work. This is the most exciting part, because **you will select and experiment with practices that fuel well-being and enliven work.**

The final chapter in this guide (**chapter 8**) invites you to revisit the Self-Reflections and ideas you've captured along the way, to imagine how it might look to live and work in a way that better supports your well-being. You'll be guided to identify replenishing routines that you want to weave into the fabric of your life and create a plan that makes those routines more sustainable.

How to Use This Guide to Chart Your Course

This guide invites you to consider the **Current** version of your well-being story and what it might look like to realize a more optimal version of that story. The process begins in chapter 2, as you define for yourself what well-being looks like for you. Building on this **Current** state, you'll be invited to imagine your **Ideal** well-being story. Don't get too hung up on the word "Ideal." This is not about perfection, but about imagining what it looks like for you to reach your highest levels of well-being given the resources and circumstances of your life. For every person, this **Ideal** well-being story looks different, and this guide invites you to determine what that means for you.

As you have already experienced in the self-reflection questions above, each chapter invites you to respond to questions and reflect on the content shared. You can use these activities to help you identify your best path towards a new way of working. You can read it through sequentially or jump to a specific chapter to get started in the area that seems to be calling to you most strongly. Feel free not to read through the whole guide at once. Take your time and carefully consider the prompts and activities. Go at your own pace, maybe reading one chapter a week, and then revisiting your responses to the **Let's Explore** sections before moving on. The **Waypoints** at the end of each chapter provide a reference point to help you know where you are and where you are going in the guide.

It might be helpful to read this guide along with a trusted friend, coach, or coworker; maybe you could weave some of the reflection questions into conversations with mentors or peers. For some people, it's easier to process the questions out loud in conversations with others. You might want to invite a group of peers or co-workers to read through the guide together and discuss the reflections or activities in a weekly or monthly book club.

Write your responses into the spaces provided. If it is easier for you to capture your thoughts digitally, then go for it! If you are a journal lover like me, use a journal.

You could schedule some time once a week to sit in a favorite chair with a soothing beverage, with a favorite soundtrack, or the sounds of nature engaging your senses. Maybe light a candle, cozy up to a fireplace, or sit in a sunbeam outside or near a window. Whether it's fifteen minutes or an hour, savor the gift of time to tune in and connect with whatever surfaces within.

A Call to Connect More Deeply with Yourself

As you work your way through the prompts and activities, try not to judge or criticize what emerges. Notice, acknowledge, and get curious. If something feels uncomfortable and you aren't ready to engage with certain thoughts, just capture them and give yourself permission to come back to them when you are ready.

Be cautious about leaping to take any specific action based on what emerges. Sometimes when an idea surfaces, you'll be filled with excitement and feel an impulse to act on it. In your life, up to this point, you might have found that immediately acting on your instincts has served you well. This is an invitation to pause before acting. When you feel compelled to take specific action as you read this guide, take a deep breath, and acknowledge the idea. What excites you? What matters most to you? Then give yourself some time to sit with it. Give yourself a pause, even if it's just a 10-minute breath practice or a walk around the block. Over time, this process of pausing and reflecting before acting might become a powerful new way of ensuring you are moving forward in alignment with what matters most to you.

In exploring an idea, it might be helpful to gather more information or data, tap into insights gained from past lessons learned, consider how actions are aligned with your values, imagine different scenarios, or look for external cues or input from others to guide you.

Pauses need not take a great deal of time. If an action does not come with life-altering implications, you might feel the freedom to experiment and take a bit of a risk. Small setbacks or failures can be incredible mechanisms for learning and growth.

Think about the first steps that an infant takes. It's a natural part of the process to take a step forward and stumble or fall. What's important is to do so with some boundaries and safeguards (e.g., taking those first steps in a carpeted room or on soft grass with an attentive caregiver nearby). At some point, you'll reach a decision point that requires a leap of faith with bigger risks. Experimenting with smaller risks and actions prepares you for the bigger leaps later. Trust that each small step brings you closer to a new way of being and to the life you once only imagined could be.

Anchors Aweigh!

Are you ready to get started on the path towards more purposeful, connected, and fulfilling work that feels aligned with and supportive of your well-being? Chapter 2 invites you to consider what it means to you to be well.

CHAPTER 1

WAYPOINTS

- This chapter invited you to identify the signs and signals in your life that indicate it might be time for something to change or be adjusted.

- Reading my wake-up call story might have reminded you of a wake-up call moment in your life.

- You reflected on the presence of any feelings of misalignment between your work and other life priorities.

- Chapter 2 will build upon these reflections and consider what it means to you to be well.

Chapter 2
Whole Person Well-Being

"What's the point of success if it doesn't bring fulfillment? Even worse, what if our current approach to success is hurting our health and moving us further away from fulfillment?"

Vivek Murthy, 19th & 21st U.S. Surgeon General

My Shift to a Broader Approach for Well-Being

I was a competitive athlete from my teen years through my early 40's and started my career as a fitness professional, so I always considered myself to be fairly healthy. But in the months leading up to my collapse and broken jaw, my family and friends began prodding me to slow down and work less. My boss told me to cut back on my overtime when I complained about how tired I was, but I felt as if I had little room to do so. I led a research department at a mid-size company and my entire workday was packed with meetings, leaving no time to respond to emails or the half dozen mini crises that came up during the day. The requests for client and sales support seemed like something I couldn't turn down and those demands often took priority over the work I needed to do to meet my own department's goals.

My individual team members also needed my guidance and support. Back then, "balance" looked like me drinking my fruit and veggie smoothies during meetings, getting up at 4 AM to run and do yoga, and responding to emails after dinner to avoid staying late at the office. Sunday afternoons were devoted to meeting prep and catching up on the backlog of email before the new week began. When family and friends asked me what was going on in my life, my response often focused on what I was doing for my work. When I explained the dilemma to my boss, she told me no one could figure this out for me. She said I needed to determine how to set boundaries and prioritize my work. I appreciated having autonomy in my work, but I was hoping for more specific guidance about what responsibilities I might let go of or for more permission to say "no" to some of the demands on my schedule. My problem was that everything felt like a high priority, and I didn't feel empowered to push back on the constant requests for client and sales support. I felt stuck.

Experimenting With Well-Being

After my wake-up call, I tried working less and cutting back on socializing on the weekends. Due to doctor's orders not to impair bone healing for my jaw, I negotiated boundaries for the number of meetings I could accept each day, making time for work in between meetings. For the first time in my 11 years with the company, I turned down client travel for eight consecutive weeks. It offered much-needed rest, but it felt temporary, and I wondered how long I'd be able to sustain and get away with these boundaries.

In the weeks and months that followed my return to work, I took a stab at changing things. I prioritized more self-care. I started reading books on happiness, doing more yoga and less running, and returned to a daily journaling practice—a practice I had stopped when writing my doctoral dissertation on top of full-time work. I also experimented with working from home on Fridays, with limited meetings, so I could catch up on work that required more mental focus.

After several months of self-reflection journaling, I began to realize that the reason I was pushing myself so hard at work—even to the point of physical collapse—was due to feelings of emptiness deep within me. Beneath the veneer of busy-ness, there was a growing sense of disengagement and lack of fulfillment. I discovered that I was trying to fill myself up by achieving one goal after another at work. After a while, each victory began to feel hollow. I felt as two-dimensional as the paper my resume was printed on.

Reflecting on this now, it seems obvious that the questions surfacing for me were typical for any mid-career professional in their forties: What is the point of the hard work? What's most important personally? Once all the major goals for education, career, and life are achieved, why do the achievements feel so empty? Is there something more than this? And perhaps most disturbing, will I ever feel deep, satisfying joy again?

The musings in my journal had me digging beneath the surface of my professional success, rigorous fitness routine, and overfull social schedule to discover my inner state. I realized that I felt isolated and lonely even though I had a large network of family and friends. I felt cynical about my work and found myself being critical and combative with coworkers I used to get along with. I knew that I needed a change, but was not sure what kind of change was needed. I suspected there were dimensions of my well-being that were not being addressed, and that was the beginning of my search for a broader view of well-being.

What Does Well-Being Mean to You?

As you'll see in the next reflection, this guide relies on the power of story. Story is a fundamental way that we humans make sense of the world and communicate about our experiences. Your story is your account of past, current, or future events. This reflection invites you to identify what well-being means for you.

Additional reflections in the chapters ahead will build on this vision and invite you to imagine what it could look like if you were living in full alignment with your greatest hope for yourself. Stories can inspire us to see beyond ourselves, connecting us to universal themes, moral principles, or a higher power. Capturing our story in journal prompts or through verbal storytelling with others is linked to emotional well-being and healing.

Self-Reflection: Your Current Well-Being Story

Think about a time in your life when you experienced the highest level of well-being you've had in your life. What did/does that look like?

Be specific by identifying the actions or behaviors involved, the circumstances of your life, and how you felt or feel physically, emotionally, and mentally.

Well-being can mean many different things to people.

Draw a picture that visualizes the things well-being represents for you now.

Don't worry about making it pretty! Doodles, symbols, and word clouds are okay.

Another way to broaden your view of well-being is to systematically assess its various domains. The Harvard Flourishing Index, developed by Harvard researchers, is used around the world to assess distinct areas of flourishing or human well-being. Let's use it to gain insight about your **Current** story.

Let's Explore: The Harvard Flourishing Index

Consider the following questions to better understand your **Current** state of well-being. Rate your **Current** level of well-being in each area using "0" as low and "10" as high.

Happiness and Life Satisfaction

1. Overall, how satisfied are you with life these days?

    0 = Not Satisfied at All   10 = Completely Satisfied   _____

2. In general, how happy or unhappy do you usually feel?

    0 = Extremely Unhappy   10 = Extremely Happy   _____

Mental and Physical Health

3. In general, how would you rate your physical health?

    0 = Poor   10 = Excellent   _____

4. In general, how would you rate your overall mental health?

    0 = Poor   10 = Excellent   _____

Meaning and Purpose

5. To what extent do you feel the things you do in your life are worthwhile?

    0 = Not at All Worthwhile   10 = Completely Worthwhile   _____

6. To what extent do you have a sense of your purpose in life?

    0 = No Sense Of Purpose   10 = Strong Sense Of Purpose   _____

Character and Virtue

7. To what extent do you act to promote good in all circumstances, even in difficult and challenging situations?

    0 = No Extent   10 = Great Extent   _____

8. To what extent are you able to give up some happiness now for greater happiness later?

    0 = No Extent   10 = Great Extent   _____

Social Connection and Relationships

9. To what extent are you content with your friendships and relationships?

0 = No Extent   10 = Great Extent   _____

10. To what extent are your relationships as satisfying as you would want them to be?

0 = No Extent   10 = Great Extent   _____

Financial and Material Stability

11. How often do you worry about being able to meet normal monthly living expenses?

0 = Worry All of the Time   10 = Do Not Ever Worry   _____

12. How often do you worry about safety, food, or housing?

0 = Worry All of the Time   10 = Do Not Ever Worry   _____

As you review the scores above, you might notice you have higher scores in some areas and lower scores in other areas. This is normal, and it's possible for you to have an overall sense of positive well-being even if some areas of your life feel more challenging right now. Let go of judgment as you consider the following additional reflections.

Which of the six areas above are associated with the highest numbers?

What do the highest areas indicate to you about Current areas of strength or resources available to you?

Harvard Flourishing Index VanderWeele TJ. "On the Promotion of Human Flourishing." *Proceedings of the National Academy of Sciences*. 2017; 31: 8148-8156. This work is licensed under a Creative Commons Attribution-NonCommercial 4.0 International License.

Which areas are of greatest importance in your life right now?

These may not necessarily be the areas with the lowest numbers for you, though the numeric scores might be a guide.

....

....

....

....

When you reflect on your Current well-being story, what might be missing?

Is there anything that feels incomplete?

....

....

....

....

Let's Explore: Your Ideal Well-Being Story

Imagine yourself **two years from now** living a life that you enjoy so much you do not need a break or an escape from it.

What does that look and feel like? How does it differ from where you are now?

....

....

....

....

....

Based on these reflections, how would you describe your Ideal story of well-being, despite any known limitations that exist for you?

_____

_____

_____

_____

_____

If you sense that there is a gap between your **Current** well-being story and the way you wish things could be, your **Ideal** well-being story, you are in the right place. I've experienced the sense of knowing that things were off course but wasn't sure how to move forward. Reflections like those above aim to help us identify potential areas for change. By the end of this guide, even if you have not made major changes in your life, working through the questions will help you consider the resources and possibilities that are open to you. Keep reading to learn more about steps you might take to gain more meaning, fulfillment, and balance in your life.

Side Trip!

If You'd Like to Spend a Little More Time Exploring

Harvard researchers have developed twelve activities that have been shown to improve these areas of flourishing. In addition to the activities in this guide, you can access the Harvard flourishing application online or through a mobile app. It's free and easy to use. See the **Resources** section for more information.

CHAPTER 2

WAYPOINTS

- This chapter invited you to reflect on what it looks like and feels like for you to experience the highest level of well-being that is possible for you.

- The Harvard Flourishing Index introduced six areas of well-being, and you reflected on areas of strength and areas of highest priority.

- You reflected on your **Current** well-being story and your **Ideal** well-being story.

- Chapter 3 invites you to consider the spiritual dimension of well-being as one potential area for exploration.

Chapter 3

The Heart and Soul of Well-Being

"We are not human beings having a spiritual experience. We are spiritual beings having a human experience."

Wayne W. Dyer, motivational author

Discovering the Missing Piece of the Well-Being Puzzle

Several years after my wake-up call, I made my way back to a place of personal and professional thriving. I reintroduced several practices that I'd let go of in the transitions between college, married life, and launching my career. I experimented with adding prayer into my daily commute, enrolling in a yoga teacher certification course to deepen my understanding of the philosophical underpinnings of the practice, and keeping a daily gratitude journal. I paid more attention to the kinds of work tasks that energized me and those that drained me, making changes where I could to shift my priorities.

After many months, I experienced a slow recovery of my previous energy and enthusiasm for my work. Encouraged by this, I contemplated doing more research on approaches to wellness that incorporated elements of spirituality. However, when I raised the idea of addressing spirituality as an aspect of my research in workforce well-being, I was discouraged from pursuing it. I continued to do research on best-practice approaches to workplace well-being but promised myself that someday I'd take a sabbatical year off and explore this interest more deeply.

Reconnecting to Spirituality

Fast forward to 2021. I'm half-way through my sabbatical year and have a call with a professional peer named Mike, who is aware that I quit my job as vice president of research in exchange for the freedom to pursue interests that were outside of the focus for my role. He's interested in catching up to learn how my planned twelve-month sabbatical is going. As I prepare for the call, I wonder how much detail to share about the topics I've focused on. I breathe a brief prayer for discernment and dial his number. We share updates about recent travel and what we're observing in our communities before the conversation turns to my sabbatical.

"I've been doing a lot of reading," I begin. "It's been a joy to follow my curiosity from one book to the next and I'm going through a book a week, on average. On the rare weeks where I don't have calls or advisory board commitments, I get through a book every day or two and I'm just loving it!"

Mike laughs. "That sounds like you. You've always been a bookworm. Is there a specific theme to your reading? What are you most curious about?"

I pause and answer the question authentically. "You might recall that in 2019, I edited a special section for the *American Journal of Health Promotion* on the topic of spiritual well-being as part of workplace well-being programs. I wanted to revisit that topic to see what's emerged in the research."

Mike is silent for a moment, then encourages me. "And what did you find?"

I take a deep breath and continue. "I was surprised to stumble upon a huge body of work related to workplace spirituality. Much of it seems to have come out of the management sciences sector. I'm not seeing much integration of this work into workforce well-being, and I've been trying to discover why. In between books, I've been interviewing consultants and thought leaders working in this space. I have a lot of discovery left to do, but I can't seem to make a dent in the number of books on my reading list. For every book I finish, there are two more referenced or recommended to me." I pause, eager for Mike's reaction.

Coming to Terms with Terms

"Well, the topic of spirituality isn't coming up in my conversations with leaders." I note his cautious tone as he continues. "I'm probably hearing more about purpose and mental health than anything. I think spirituality is a big turn-off for leaders in the business world because their mind immediately leaps to religion and there's the whole separation of church and state issue in the back of their minds. If you decide to focus on this work, I recommend using different terms when you talk to business leaders about it."

It's been several years since this conversation with Mike, and since then I have put a lot of thought into how I broach the topic of spirituality in my conversations with professional peers and business leaders. As much as I'm encouraged by the growing body of research that supports spirituality as an essential domain of well-being, it can be a loaded word for some people. The next set of reflection questions invite you to consider your own views and feelings about this term, and then I'll share what I learned about the importance of this dimension during my sabbatical year.

Self-Reflection: Your Views on Spirituality

What brings you the most meaning, hope, comfort, and inner peace in your life and how do you experience this?

....

....

....

What practices or activities help you to feel the most grounded and connected to your innermost self?

☐ Life events including births, deaths, weddings, or graduation days

☐ Listening to music that inspires feelings of peace

☐ Volunteering for a meaningful cause

☐ Taking a walk in nature and pausing to admire its beauty

☐ Offering or receiving kindness and compassion

☐ Connecting with others in book groups or on your own

☐ Singing, dancing, and/or praying that connects to something higher than yourself

☐ Visiting a loved one who is ill or homebound

☐ Cooking with friends and mindfully eating the food

☐ Taking a yoga class and connecting to your breathing

☐ Meditation practices

☐ Journaling

☐ Expressing gratitude

☐ Helping someone in need or serving others

☐ Other activities:

What words would you use to describe what it means to be spiritual?

....

....

....

Recall a time when you felt at your most spiritual.

What about this memory/time led you to feel it was spiritual?

How does religion fit into your view of what it means to be spiritual?

Distinguishing Between Spirituality and Religion

Even though there are thousands of published articles and studies in the field of spirituality, there is a lack of consensus about definitions and distinctions between religion, faith, and spirituality among experts. Hundreds of studies demonstrate a link between spirituality/religion and healthier lifestyles, mental and physical health outcomes, longer life, and higher perceived quality of life.

The Fetzer Institute has been studying how people think about spirituality and religion for the past several years. They've used focus groups, surveys, and individual interviews to understand how adults in the United States distinguish between spirituality and religion. Here's what they found.

> *"...spirituality is a complex, diverse, and nuanced phenomenon that people of all spiritual and religious self-identifications experience...it is human to be spiritual, and engaging in this spirituality can engender a greater good."*

The American Academy of Family Physicians definition for spirituality may be helpful to you.

> **Spirituality** is the way you find meaning, hope, comfort and inner peace in your life. Many people find spirituality through religion. Some find it through music, art, or a connection with nature. Others find it in their values and principles.

Others describe spirituality this way:

> **Spirituality** is the aspect of humanity that refers to the way individuals seek and express meaning and purpose and the way they experience their connectedness to the moment, to self, to others, to nature, and to the significant or sacred.

Without using a specific definition, Fetzer's ongoing research found **more than eight out of ten people consider themselves spiritual to some extent and nearly half aspire to be more spiritual.** When study participants were asked how they most frequently expressed their spirituality, they named prayer, yoga or other kinds of mindful movement, reading, being in nature, and participating in the arts (singing, painting, making music).

It's important to acknowledge that for some people, spirituality includes some reference to the divine, while others might perceive themselves to be deeply spiritual without believing in the presence of the divine or following a specific faith tradition. **The path forward does not require us to agree on a single universal definition of spirituality, but rather to recognize it is an essential part of what it means to be human.** Spirituality provides individuals with a sense of identity, wholeness, satisfaction, joy, contentment, beauty, love, respect, positive attitudes, inner peace and harmony, and purpose and direction in life.

As I've reviewed the many ways that researchers measure and define spirituality, it often addresses connection at three different levels, including a deeper sense of connection with our purpose; with other people (social connection); and to something bigger than ourselves (transcendence). Part Two of this guide will address each one of these areas in turn. Before we explore these three areas further, let's consider how spirituality fits with a whole person approach to well-being.

Spirituality as a Dimension of Whole Person Well-Being

Spiritual well-being has long been on the radar in the world of wellness. In fact, it was included in the National Wellness Institute's 1976 seminal model, which names six areas of well-being and includes spirituality among them. Ten years after that model was published, the *American Journal of Health Promotion* called for health promotion practitioners to include spirituality in their organizations' wellness initiatives. It's taken time for this idea to be adopted, but leading organizations point the way forward. In recent years, the US Army has been taking a data driven approach to developing the "whole soldier." They looked at 25 years of peer reviewed research, concluding that a strong spiritual core is the hub of a wheel for a whole healthy person with or without religion. Researchers at Gallup have identified five factors of spirituality that influence well-being, including positive coping and a sense of purpose in life, faith-based social connection, community/civic engagement, structural stability, and workplace support of holistic well-being.

Religion is one of the things we sometimes leave out of our work and other settings because it's seen as a contentious issue. In the US, there are laws that protect workers from religious discrimination and lay ground rules for how to accommodate workers whose religious beliefs influence their behaviors at work. Such laws may cause organizations to tread carefully. While some organizations are recognized as being "faith friendly" or "faith focused," there are others that discourage any expression of religious or faith beliefs at work. There is a need to differentiate religion from spirituality because spirituality is an essential dimension in a whole person approach to well-being. Though broaching spirituality at work requires some sensitivity, researchers from the McKinsey Health Institute suggest the workplace can be a place where people experience a strong sense of purpose (one of cornerstones of spirituality). In addition, university settings have long included spirituality in their approach to workforce well-being and serve as examples for other organizations to follow.

Self-Reflection: How Important is the Spiritual Dimension to You?

To what extent do you consider yourself to be a *spiritual* person?
- ☐ Very
- ☐ Moderately
- ☐ Slightly
- ☐ Not At All

To what extent do you consider yourself to be a *religious* person?
- ☐ Very
- ☐ Moderately
- ☐ Slightly
- ☐ Not At All

In what ways is it important or unimportant for you to be able to express these aspects of yourself with your friends, family, or coworkers?

Review your **Current** well-being story from page **21** of this guide.

Based on the information about spirituality in this chapter, which aspects show up in your Current well-being story?

What aspects of spirituality would you consider incorporating into your Ideal well-being story?

Now that you've considered what a whole person approach to well-being might look like for you, keep reading to explore how work can have an influence on your well-being.

CHAPTER 3

WAYPOINTS

- This chapter introduced the spiritual dimension of well-being and invited you to consider what this means for you.

- While there is not a single consensus definition of spirituality, most researchers agree it is an essential aspect of being human.

- Spirituality encompasses religion but it is possible to be spiritual without being religious or believing in the existence of the Divine. More than 8 out of 10 people self-identify as being spiritual to some extent.

- The next chapter invites you to consider the role of work as an influence on your well-being.

Chapter 4
Work and Your Well-Being

"It's not how much money we make that ultimately makes us happy between 9 and 5. It's whether or not our work fulfills us."

Malcolm Gladwell, author

Ten years ago, I started the habit of taking one-on-one meetings and calls that did not require sitting at my computer as a walking meeting. I encouraged my family members and professional peers to do the same. It's one of many ways that I have integrated well-being into my largely sedentary work as a writer and researcher. Several months after my conversation with Mike about my sabbatical focus, I am walking on my treadmill in time to take a call with my friend, David, who is also eschewing the video call for a walking meeting.

David and I are enrolled in an online course about navigating mid-life transitions, and he confided to me several months ago, that he was considering a job change from a somewhat operational director role to a more strategic role in the health and well-being space. After an initial catch-up on lighter topics, I shift the conversation into deeper territory by asking how things are going with his work.

"Funny you should ask," David replies. "I just happen to have a meeting with my executive leaders at the end of the day. I'd like to give my resignation."

"What?!" I can't keep the surprise out of my voice and nearly trip while walking on the treadmill. I slow the pace a bit and regain my composure before saying in a more neutral tone, "I know you've been considering a job change. What precipitated today's meeting?"

David tells me about a series of communications he's had in recent weeks and how he's feeling the senior executive team has not been taking his recommendations about needing to address staff well-being more seriously. "You know, I took this job because I thought the leaders in this organization were serious about investing in the health and well-being of their workers, but every time I make a recommendation, they make some excuse about it not being the right time. On the heels of the latest corporate directive to launch another initiative focused on bolstering market share, I am at the point where this work no longer feels aligned with the work I want to be doing. I requested this meeting to start discussions about transitioning out of the organization."

As we continue our conversation, I reflect on a pattern I've seen emerging among my peer group over the past several years. David is one of at least a dozen professional peers in senior leadership roles who initiated a departure from their organization because its direction was not aligned with their personal values or met their needs for professional fulfillment. In addition to those, I know several peers who are burned out and are looking to take a break to recover their energy and strength. David's story reminds me of the dissatisfaction I had experienced in my career when I felt my work wasn't making a meaningful difference in the world. Unlike David, I wasn't ready to quit my job. If you feel that way too, there is a lot you can do to find more meaning and fulfillment in your work without quitting your job.

Self-Reflection: The Influence of Work on Your Well-Being

Consider the role of your work in your life. Generally speaking, how does work contribute to or diminish your sense of well-being?

How do your personal and professional goals support your well-being goals? Are there any ways they work against each other?

Refer back to your scores on the **Harvard Flourishing Index** on pages **22-23**. For easy reference, copy your scores here:

Happiness and Life Satisfaction

1. Overall, how satisfied are you with life these days? _____

2. In general, how happy or unhappy do you usually feel? _____

Mental and Physical Health

3. In general, how would you rate your physical health? _____

4. In general, how would you rate your overall mental health? _____

Meaning and Purpose

5. To what extent do you feel the things you do in your life are worthwhile?
_____

6. To what extent do you have a sense of your purpose in life? _____

Character and Virtue

7. To what extent do you act to promote good in all circumstances, even in difficult and challenging situations? _____

8. To what extent are you able to give up some happiness now for greater happiness later? _____

Social Connection and Relationships

9. To what extent are you content with your friendships and relationships?
_____

10. To what extent are your relationships as satisfying as you would want them to be? _____

Financial and Material Stability

11. How often do you worry about being able to meet normal monthly living expenses? _____

12. How often do you worry about safety, food, or housing? _____

As you review your recorded scores:

Identify one area where your work *contributes positively* **to your well-being. In what ways does your work help you feel vital, energized, and fulfilled?**

Identify one area where your work *threatens or diminishes* **your well-being? In what ways does your work leave you feeling drained, disengaged, or depleted?**

If you struggled to name specific ways that work influences your well-being, this list may help. It identifies common drivers of well-being at work.

Check the items in the list that are true for you and feel free to name a few of your own.

- ☐ Feeling a sense of pride in my organization's purpose
- ☐ Having fulfilling work
- ☐ Having a sense of belonging with my coworkers
- ☐ Feeling valued at work
- ☐ Having fun at work
- ☐ Having a manager who advocates for me
- ☐ Having access to technology that makes my job easier
- ☐ Having organizational support for a healthy lifestyle
- ☐ Other drivers:

This is an incomplete list, reflecting only the top drivers of employee thriving identified by researchers at Mercer. You might be asking yourself how it's possible for work to have a more positive impact on your sense of well-being. For now, know that fulfilling work and feeling valued at work are consistently identified in research as contributors to our well-being.

What the Research Tells Us

Well-being is not an outcome or a goal that you achieve once. It's informed by a dynamic interplay of life circumstances, our environment, and our everyday actions. Since we spend so much of our waking time engaged in our work, the workplace has a tremendous influence on our well-being. Unfortunately, employee perceptions about their state of well-being are at their lowest levels since Gallup researchers started measuring it globally in 2009. Despite executive leaders naming employee well-being as one of their top three priorities in 2024, employee mental and emotional well-being trends continue to decline. Gartner research indicates 82% of employees want their organizations to see them as a whole person, but only 45% report feeling their organization views them this way. What's more, only about half of all employees find their jobs fulfilling or feel that they can be themselves at work.

When you ask people what contributes to a fulfilling life, 71% of all adults say having a job or career they enjoy is extremely or very important for a fulfilling life. Nearly as many (61%) say having close friends is equally important. These rank above having a lot of money, being married, or having children—things commonly named as contributing to having a fulfilling life. Gallup research confirms that having enough money to meet our basic needs is essential for our well-being and happiness, but there is a threshold where more money fails to satisfy our deepest needs.

Defining Work from a Spiritual Perspective

Traditional definitions of work often emphasize compensation, productivity, effort, and employment. However, work can also be understood as a spiritual endeavor, an expression of one's purpose, values, and connection to something greater than oneself. Work is not merely a means of earning a living, but a pathway for personal growth, service, and transcendence.

> **Work** can be defined as a meaningful expression of one's purpose, values, and relationships, with the intention and integrity to contribute to the greater good.

This definition moves beyond an economic perspective, highlighting the role of work to advance a personal purpose in life, nurture meaningful social connection with others, and engage in acts of service that connect with something greater than oneself (transcendence). You'll recall from chapter 3, that these were the three aspects of spirituality identified in my review of the research during my sabbatical.

Does The Workplace Deliver?

It used to be enough for organizations to offer a competitive salary, a safe place to work, and some employee health and well-being benefits, but employees are now demanding more in return for the time, effort, and intellectual capital they bring to their employers. They want to be valued for their contributions and ". . . to be seen as complex human beings with rich, full lives." Workers in a variety of positions from hourly nail technicians to specialty practice physicians are leaving their jobs in search of a more enriching life. Many individuals leave traditional workplaces to pursue work independently or on a volunteer basis. The desire for a better environment can be a contributing factor.

Journalist, Adam Chandler, argues in his book *99% Perspiration: A New Working History of the American Way of Life* that contemporary American work standards are damaging employee well-being. Sustained excessive workload and lack of control in one's job are just two factors contributing to work-related stress and burnout. A toxic workplace culture is a third contributor, characterized by office gossip, sexism, bullying, and incivility at work. According to research by the Society of Human Resource Management, workers in the United States alone collectively experience more than 223 million acts of incivility every day. This includes rudeness, dismissiveness, unresponsiveness, aggression, or coworkers taking credit for others' work. Such behaviors are associated with increased levels of stress, emotional exhaustion, burnout, and depression. Burnout levels also continue to be at extremely high levels.

At Risk for Burnout

One 2024 global survey estimates 81% of workers are at risk for burnout within the next year, with two in five workers believing "the world of work is fundamentally broken."

There is increasing attention on the role of business leaders to address these issues in the workplace. When I initially began review of research on workplace spirituality, I discovered links to servant leadership, conscious leadership, and enlightened leadership. This guide does not aim to identify the behaviors and practices that leaders can influence to support whole person well-being (see my 2022 book for more information). However, if you are in a formal or informal leadership role, you are also a human being, and effective leadership requires an investment in your own well-being.

While organizational and managerial efforts are crucial in addressing these threats to employee well-being, there are steps we can take as individuals to bolster and protect our own well-being. Sometimes this requires we seek professional support or take advantage of resources offered by our employer or community that are designed to address specific challenges or problems. You're nearly done with Part One of this guide, which means you've already made a substantial investment in your own well-being.

Continue with a final reflection about how the workplace environment can influence well-being and to identify where you might want to explore additional resources to support your own well-being.

Self-Reflection: Identify Needs for Additional Support

Which of these areas might you need to explore further as part of realizing your Ideal well-being story?

*Place a check in the boxes next to all that you would include. Then, write numbers in the margin to prioritize the **top three** things.*

☐ **Burnout:** Recognize the signs of burnout in yourself and identify workplace contributors

☐ **Workload/Stress:** Evaluate/discuss workload and stress levels with supervisor, family members, or other influencers (such as volunteer organizations, friends, other dependents)

☐ **Work-Life Boundaries:** Create clear separation or balance between work and life activities or improve "focus time" for each

☐ **Self Care:** Improve your quality of sleep, regular exercise, diet, and breaks/rest

☐ **Stress Management:** Add recovery and renewal practices such as mindfulness, meditation, or other relaxation techniques to release stress and tension at regular intervals (e.g., breaks after stressful conversations, after physical exertion, after errands/commute, before sleep)

☐ **Social Support Communities:** Build relationships with peers who share specific challenges you face or join a support community facilitated by a health professional

☐ **Professional Help:** Engage a mental health professional, an Employee Assistance Program (EAP), a professional life coach, or medical help

We will revisit the items you checked here and the priority you placed on them in the latter part of this guide. **Mark this page**. We're coming back to it!

Side Trip!

If You'd Like to Spend a Little More Time Exploring

The areas above represent significant challenges to our well-being. Global statistics indicate that, at some point, most of us struggle with one or more of these issues as part of our work. The strategies identified in this guide can fill a gap not addressed by existing resources and can complement traditional resources that support mental, emotional, and occupational well-being. See the **Resources** section for information and tools that more directly address some of the challenges identified above.

If you are currently working with a behavioral health professional or coach, you might wish to share your priorities and insights from this section and discuss any actions you wish to take.

The rest of this guide will address broader well-being needs that support resilience and a preventive approach to mental and emotional well-being issues. The **Let's Explore** sections will help you connect with your own inner wisdom to identify where course corrections may be needed.

CHAPTER 4

WAYPOINTS

- This chapter invited you to reflect on the influence of work on your well-being, both as a positive contributor and as a threat.

- You reflected on how your personal and professional goals are aligned or unaligned, and what contributes to your well-being at work.

- You identified areas where you might need additional support to complement the discovery and exploration exercises in this guide.

- You've completed the first part of the guide to *Get Your Bearings*. Part Two of this guide will help you *Chart Your Course* towards more purposeful, connected, and transcendent work.

PART TWO

Chart Your Course

The Self-Reflections and activities that follow in Part Two of this guide are intended to help you identify:

- Core beliefs about who you are and what you are meant to do
- What matters most to you in life
- Your most cherished core values
- How you want to show up in the world
- Who matters most to you
- What brings you joy
- Activities that leave you feeling most fulfilled
- Replenishing routines that you want to weave into your daily life
- New patterns of working that support whole person well-being

The next few chapters will build on and more deeply examine your **Current** story of well-being, identify ways to address what's missing, and continue to visualize your **Ideal** well-being story. In addition to work life, there are many cultural/external factors that influence the ability to be well anywhere. Defining your **Ideal** story and creating awareness of your **Current** story, are steps that give you power to make the changes you want for yourself.

Resources are provided at the end of the chapters to dive deeper into specific areas. You may be drawn to practices that you have not recognized or used before. Take opportunities to explore what's available from credible non-profit organizations, your employer, community organizations, or faith community.

Keep these things in mind as we move into the next section of the guide, which addresses each of the following core aspects of spirituality: purpose; social connection, and transcendence.

Chapter 5
Purpose (Connect to Self)

"If one does not know to which port one is sailing, no wind is favorable."

Seneca, philosopher

In my own quest to identify the gaps between my **Current** well-being story and my **Ideal** well-being story, I came across a leadership training program called *The Corporate Athlete*, which was developed by the Human Performance Institute. It was an intensive, three-and-a-half-day retreat and I was eager to go. Several of my professional peers in other companies had attended and said it was transformative. I was particularly intrigued by its inclusion of spirituality in their published model. My employer didn't support leadership training programs like this, and I didn't know how to approach my boss about going. I thought about paying my own way, but it was too expensive for me to cover on my own. I sat on the information for more than a year before I found an opening during a meeting with my boss.

During my annual performance review, my boss asked me about my future goals, specifically if I had any desire to take a higher-level executive role in a company. I answered him honestly: I'd learned through many months of reflection what I enjoyed and didn't enjoy about my work. I realized that I disliked the more administrative and operational aspects of my job and was concerned that an executive position would take me away from conducting research and writing (two of my favorite work activities). He wanted to know how to support me in my professional growth and that's when I told him about the leadership retreat. Several months later, he told me that he'd put in a request for me to attend the training as a reward for meeting my performance goals year over year. It was approved! I immediately booked the next available training, which was at a resort about ninety minutes away.

Approaching Myself with Truth

Preparatory work leading up to the training included a 360-degree assessment; my superiors, peers within the company, peers outside of the company, family members, and employees who reported to me completed a survey about me. I also completed several self-assessments.

As I reviewed the feedback results in the week prior to the retreat, I started to question the wisdom of signing up for the program. In nearly all cases, the personalized report based on the 360-degree assessment revealed that my behaviors at work, at home, and in my social circles did not align with the values that I said were most important to me in my self-assessment. For example, I wasn't attending church, yet I counted my faith as a core part of my identity. I didn't feel like I could express that part of my identity in my professional life, but there was a desire within me to live out my values more in my work. As I reviewed my top values in the report, I knew my tendency to swear and drink more heavily around certain people was counter to who I believed I was. A key element of this training included facing these truths.

I experienced mounting anxiety in the days leading up to the training as I realized it was time to face the truth about the lack of alignment between my core beliefs and my behaviors. I might have to make more significant changes in my life to better align my ways of working with my values. Yikes! What had I gotten myself into?

A Pivotal Waypoint in My Journey

The evening before the opening session of the retreat, I wrote a pep talk to myself in my journal. I affirmed to myself this was something I knew was part of the program. I'd mentioned the training program to my boss because I knew, deep down, this was inner work I had to do. As uncomfortable as it was, this was the time and space to imagine a new way of working.

The next few days were a combination of classroom-style teaching, break-out conversations with our assigned cohort groups, one-on-one coaching, and hours of self-reflective journal exercises. During the first two days, we identified a purpose statement for our lives and prioritized our core values. Based on our purpose and core values, we developed a storyline that detailed the way we lived our lives against them and then crafted a desired future story. Using the results of the 360-degree assessment, we detailed what specific behaviors needed to change in every aspect of our lives to support our purpose and align our behaviors with our values. From there, we created a ninety-day plan for how we'd embed new or replacement behaviors and practices into our lives and identify accountability partners with whom we could share our intentions. This transformative experience is what compelled me to include the power of story into this guide.

That retreat happened more than ten years ago and as I look back through my journals, I see how it was a game changer in terms of my overall well-being. Before the training, I struggled with work-life balance and occasionally felt depleted and disengaged at work. For example, although I knew how to live a healthy lifestyle, I often turned to overconsumption of comfort food, wine, shopping, television, or exotic vacations overseas as coping mechanisms. It took several years for me to bridge the gap between the well-being story I was living and the future Ideal story that I dreamed about. In the years since then, I've continued to pay attention to my purpose and values, refining them.

Self-Reflection: What Matters Most To You?

What behaviors or actions (rather than intentions or aspirations) reflect your top priorities in life right now? (Current story)

_____

_____

_____

Consider your values. They influence how we show up in the world, our interactions with others, and our priorities. The extent to which we live (and work) in alignment with our values influences our sense of inner peace and fulfillment.

> **Values** are a set of core beliefs and principles that shape our behaviors and guide our decisions.

As you think about the best version of yourself, your core values most represent the decision making and behaviors you'd like to see.

Underline your top 10 most important values. Feel free to add values that are not on this list (it's an incomplete list).

Achievement	Friendships	Relationships
Appreciation	Fun	Reputation
Compassion	Growth	Responsibility
Community	Honesty	Service
Creativity	Hope	Self-Control
Education	Humility	Spirituality
Empathy	Independence	Status
Enjoyment of life	Kindness	Tolerance
Excellence	Love	Trustworthiness
Expertise	Loyalty	Vitality (health)
Faith	Peace	Wealth

Circle the 3 values that most support your Ideal well-being story.

Your Ideal Story: Based on your top 3 values, create a set of statements about how you want to "show up" in the world. Use statements that describe how you wish to "be."

Ideally, I wish to be ...

Value statement 1:

....

....

Value statement 2:

....

....

Value statement 3:

....

....

Consider a typical day. Living out your values should be embedded into the things you already do, but in a way that reflects how you wish to be.

Example: Living Out Values

Value Statement: Ideally, I wish to be more kind.

Living out this value looks like:

- *Really listening to others when I ask how they are doing*
- *Taking care of unpleasant tasks with an attitude of loving service rather than griping about it*
- *Pausing to show warmth (smiling or using their name in greeting) rather than scrolling through email*

Try it. For each of your value statements, describe what it looks like to live out each value in your daily life, with all its pressures and competing demands.

Living Out My Values

Value Statement 1:

Living out this value looks like:

-
-
-
-

Value Statement 2:

Living out this value looks like:

-
-
-
-

Value Statement 3:

Living out this value looks like:

-
-
-
-

What It Means to Have a Sense of Purpose

Having a life purpose is about having a strong sense of direction for one's life. It provides an overarching aspiration that energizes our efforts and serves as a central source of meaning and significance in our lives. At its most basic level, it helps us answer life's big questions: "Why am I here?", "What am I living for?", and "What matters most to me?" At a deeper, more developed level, it identifies what in the world breaks your heart and motivates you to explore. It draws upon your innate gifts, talents, and strengths to contribute to your well-being and that of others. It is operationalized through activities that engage you in such a way that you fully immerse yourself in what you are doing, and it represents your most enduring principles and values.

> **Purpose** is a strong sense of direction for one's life; an overarching aspiration that energizes one's efforts and provides a central source of meaning and significance.

Living a purposeful life adds meaning to our everyday moments. Even the dullest tasks can be meaningful. Years ago, when I was working with a large manufacturing organization, an employee working on the medical tape manufacturing line said she tried to think about how the tape would be used to promote healing for others, and it inspired her to do her best at her job. That's what a strong sense of purpose adds to one's life. Life viewed through the lens of purpose can be more fulfilling and satisfying because it contributes to hope for the future and can help us overcome big and small challenges to resilience.

Dr. Victor J. Strecher's book, *Life on Purpose*, talks about purpose as having "a higher-order goal that has deep value" and outlines strategies for developing a personal purpose statement. His was one of the first books I read to deepen my own purpose after the Human Performance Institute training. Life purpose statements are often aspirational and may not be attainable in one's lifetime. Our life purpose might be broad and work itself out differently across the different life roles that we have. We may develop different purpose statements for different roles in our lives, and we need to keep them in balance because an overemphasis on career purpose and goals can diminish attention to family, friends, community, and personal purpose. Strecher suggests we set limits or boundaries that allow us to direct our energy and attention to our multiple purposes and to create connections between purposes. For example, participating in a work-sponsored community volunteer program may serve a career purpose and a community involvement purpose. Involving one's family and friends in that volunteerism may also contribute to relational purpose. The more we can align and integrate our multiple purposes, the less strain we feel making tradeoffs to balance them.

When it comes to identifying our life purpose, it can be helpful to think about our legacy and how we want to be remembered by others. For example, if you aspire to act with compassion and kindness toward others, your purpose statement might be, "My purpose in life is to act with compassion and kindness by considering others' needs before my own." It helps to think about what matters most in life and how that reflects our deepest values. If family is a top value and you strive to achieve a healthier work-life balance, your purpose statement might be, "My purpose in life is to be a supportive mother and partner, so I prioritize and protect family time on evenings and weekends."

Self-Reflection: Clarify Your Sense of Purpose

To what extent do you agree or disagree with the following statement?

"I have a sense of purpose and direction in my life."

- ☐ Strongly Agree
- ☐ Agree
- ☐ Somewhat Agree
- ☐ Somewhat Disagree
- ☐ Disagree
- ☐ Strongly Disagree

What does it mean to you to have a sense of purpose for your life?

What is increasingly important to you, perhaps beyond your everyday work?

How aligned do you believe your daily actions are with your sense of purpose?

If someone else observed your life, how would they describe you, and how does this align with your purpose?

A Grand Purpose Statement is Not Required for Your Life to Feel Purposeful

If it feels challenging to articulate a clear statement about a single purpose for your life, here's the good news: you don't need a grand life purpose statement for your life to feel purposeful! Living life with a sense of purpose is an evolving process. This process includes reflecting regularly on the extent to which your lifestyle and working style align with your values and what matters most to you. I used to think I had to have one grand purpose statement and that it ideally needed to align with my work. I've moved away from that thinking as I've become more familiar with the research about purpose and its importance for well-being. I've transitioned from a focus on ego-oriented achievement goals to identity-based "be" goals that focus more on how I want to show up in the world.

> **Ego-oriented goals** focus on achievement through doing, solving, accomplishing, tracking – all the things the old me thrived on!

> **Be-oriented goals** focus on the behaviors and approaches we employ to accomplish what we do.

You may find yourself establishing and then revising values and purpose in these chapters as you more fully understand and crystallize your **Ideal** story. That's okay. The work of purpose is ongoing and here's more good news: you get to change it over time!

Identifying your purpose is about articulating what you care most about and why. As you consider what matters most to you, an image may come to mind or a relationship. Certain words or phrases may surface. The key is to identify what they are for you and to intentionally point your energy toward living that purpose in your daily life.

As I reflect on the burnout, exhaustion, and lack of fulfillment I experienced earlier in my career, I realize I had lost sight of the broader meaning of my work. What I know now is that our sense of purpose often evolves as we get older. In fact, anytime we are going through significant transition or change, it's natural for questions about purpose to surface. If you are feeling less engaged in your work or less satisfied than you used to, it might be helpful to spend some time connecting with your purpose and values. Speaking from experience, it can be tempting to want to jump into a new job opportunity without fully understanding what might be contributing to the desire to leave. Pause to consider what drew you to the job or role in the first place. What may have changed in your life or contributed to new perspectives about fulfillment and meaning for you? It may be possible to remain in your role or organization by examining purpose as a key to incorporating new aspects into your work life.

Side Trip!

If You'd Like to Spend a Little More Time Exploring
You've completed a lot of reflections about what matters most to you and how you want to show up in the world. Check out the **Resources** section to go deeper in some of these areas.

Let's Explore: Deepen Your Sense of Purpose

Some suggest that purpose is a journey and a practice rather than a destination. Understanding that purpose and values can change for individuals over time requires that we build pauses and other mechanisms into our lives to revisit our sense of purpose. This is especially helpful to ensure we are living in alignment with what matters most to us.

Which of these practices can you use to reinforce your sense of purpose?

- ☐ Print out your purpose words, images, or statement. Post it somewhere so that you'll see it.
- ☐ Save an image related to your purpose as a screen saver on your computer/phone.
- ☐ Get a stone with a word engraved on it that reminds you about your purpose and use it as a paperweight at work.
- ☐ Start each day with a 10 to 15-minute review of your calendar and identify opportunities to live in alignment with your purpose and values.
- ☐ Create a vision board that depicts what it looks like to live out your purpose.
- ☐ Build accountability relationships that include checking in on how aligned you are with your purpose and values.
- ☐ Create a personal scorecard that identifies key behaviors that are observable and measurable. Create metrics that help you know how aligned your behaviors are with your purpose.
- ☐ Reflect on ways to approach your work from a mindset of purpose.

Create a Purposeful Practice

- Identify one practice from the list above.
- Create a Commitment Statement that generates excitement and anticipation.
- Give yourself a timeline for completing the practice.

Example Commitment Statement:

Move framed pictures of people I care most about next to my primary workspace. Spend 5 minutes in the morning reflecting on how to best invest in those relationships in the day ahead.

CHAPTER 5

WAYPOINTS

- This chapter focuses on the role of purpose to help you align your energy with what matters most to you in life.

- You reflected on your values and identified your top 3 values that support your Ideal well-being story.

- You were invited to clarify your sense of purpose and explore ways to deepen your sense of purpose through your work.

- Reflections on what matters most to us often surfaces thoughts about the people in our lives who are most important to us. The next chapter considers how our relationships support our well-being, including our relationships with our co-workers.

Chapter 6
Social Connection (Connect with Others)

"Connection is the energy that is created between
people when they feel seen, heard, and valued;
when they can give and receive without judgment."

Brené Brown, author, researcher, educator

A Baseline for Connection

Every one of us differs in terms of our perceived desire or need for connection, but it's biologically hardwired into us to seek it. As I consider when I first noticed a gap between the level of connection I wanted to have, and my actual experience of it, I leap back in time to the beginning of my professional career. The year is 1997. I am two years into my first professional job and I'm sitting through a performance review with my supervisor. I have worked hard and met all my project deadlines, so I am expecting a favorable performance review. Maybe even a raise! Things open on a positive note as my supervisor recognizes my reliability in completing my assigned tasks and expresses appreciation for the extra projects I've taken on in the past year. I beam with pride as he shares the feedback.

"Overall, you work hard and the others on the team know they can depend on you to get your work done. They feel more comfortable working with you now compared to in the past and say you seem more relaxed and friendly. You've contributed to some solid process improvement projects this past year and did a great job of coordinating the new classes we offered."

An Unexpected Turn

Things take an unexpected turn when we get to the portion of the review focused on professional improvement. Clearing his throat, my supervisor continues, "When it comes to doing your assigned job and completing tasks, you are doing terrific. But outcomes are not the only thing that matter. The thing you need to focus on for the year ahead is how you go about executing your work. Based on team feedback, you can come off as intimidating and controlling. When things don't go according to plan, you appear to get frustrated and irritable. You are impatient. When I am not around, they feel you are bossy and overpowering."

My supervisor lays down the piece of paper he's been reading and looks up, removing his reading glasses. "Look, I know this feedback is hard to take but I have to say I agree with the team on much of this. Overall, you are completing your job responsibilities well, but you do need to work on how you execute. Would you be open to developing a more team-oriented approach over the next year?"

My mouth is so dry I can hardly respond. I take a sip of water as I try to formulate a reply. "I have to say, I'm surprised to hear my co-workers feel this way. I am not trying to be intimidating or controlling. I don't want to be unpleasant to work with. I really care about my job and want to do well. I'm not sure what I can do differently." I look down at my hands, too ashamed to look him in the eye.

"That's a step in the right direction to want to change what you are doing. As I said, you've done an exemplary job meeting your goals. We need to shift some of that energy from what you are doing to how work gets done."

This feedback early in my career blindsided me because nothing in my academic or professional training addressed relationship building at work.

Behaviors Before Outcomes

At school and at work, the focus tended to be on outcomes. Meet the project goals and move on. While I eventually learned how to work more collaboratively as a team player, I struggled for years to figure out how to deepen my relationships at work. The good news is you don't have to struggle to figure this out. This chapter shares the guidance I wish I'd had more than 30 years ago.

Self-Reflection: Your Baseline for Social Connection

Where are opportunities to connect with others meaningfully outside of work?

- ☐ Sports I am involved in or support
- ☐ Recreation groups
- ☐ Hobby groups/events
- ☐ Volunteer roles, events, or committees
- ☐ Parent groups
- ☐ Support groups
- ☐ What else?

How important is it <u>to you</u> to have friendships at work? Choose one.

- o Extremely Important
- o Very Important
- o Moderately Important
- o Slightly Important
- o A Little Important
- o Not At All Important

How connected do you feel with those you interact with as part of your work?

- ☐ I know many people by name.
- ☐ Many people at work know my name.
- ☐ I know people from other departments, outside of my direct team.
- ☐ I know about people's interests, hobbies, or background.
- ☐ I know enough about the people I see often to ask them about what is going on in their lives and not just about their work.

Think about the last few days and your interactions at work. When did you feel most seen, heard, or valued and what circumstances contributed to it?

If you are disappointed with the quality of connections you've made this week, what is disappointing about it?

The Meaning of Social Connection

Connection has become a bit of a loaded word in modern times because we've never been so highly networked with others while being able to mask our true selves. Digital technology allows us to talk, text, tweet, message, or video chat at the push of a button. Communication strategies abound with the choice of asynchronous or real-time exchanges. Social media platforms enable us to become acquainted with hundreds of thousands of people all over the world and judge the quality of their posts with a thumbs-up or thumbs-down. The world of avatars allows us to present ourselves to others as we'd most like them to see us, with the editing features on our phones or computer cameras ensuring we're angled, lit, and cropped in the most aesthetically pleasing way. Despite the plethora of communication mechanisms available to us and access to anyone with a digital device, we've never been lonelier or felt more disconnected. According to a 2024 poll of US adults, one in three say they feel lonely at least once a week, and 10% say they feel lonely every day.

> **Social connection** relates to the state of being in relationship with others who leave you feeling seen, heard, and valued, providing a sense of support and belonging.

Connection and Belonging at Work Matter

Carl Jung's work in psychology in the early 1900's was the first to create persona archetypes for "extraverts" and "introverts." Extraverts are described as people who are more outgoing, talkative, assertive, and bold. Introverts describe people who are on the opposite end of the spectrum and present as shy, quiet, and private. His work has been developed to form the baseline of many personality and workstyle preference assessments including the Myers-Briggs Type Indicator, DiSC, and many others. This can be important in understanding that people's needs for connection vary widely. Whether you identify as introverted or extroverted, social connection is essential for our well-being.

The Importance of Social Connection

I used to think my relationships at work didn't matter if I got along with my coworkers and achieved project goals. But they do matter for your work and for your well-being.

> *When it comes to your well-being, social connection is as important as quitting smoking and maintaining your weight!*

Higher levels of social connection are associated with higher levels of physical, mental, and emotional well-being because we tend to take better care of ourselves when we feel cared for and supported. Higher levels of social support are linked to smoking cessation and medication adherence, better brain functioning, less depression, and greater life satisfaction.

This research translates into higher levels of performance at work. One study of employees working in a long-term care setting found that when employees felt affection, compassion, and caring from their coworkers, their patients benefited from better patient mood, quality of life, satisfaction with care, and a decrease in future trips to the emergency room. Social support at work has a buffering effect, mitigating the effects of stress and reducing risk of burnout.

Other studies observe the implications for health and well-being where there is a lack of social connection. Evidence links chronic loneliness with increased likelihood of dementia, cognitive decline, immunity issues, and heart disease, contributing to a shorter lifespan.

> *When people feel lonlier, they are more sensitive to negative interactions at work, perceiving these interactions to be stressful.*

One published review found that lonely individuals are more likely to interpret hostile intent, expect rejection, evaluate themselves and their co-workers negatively, and have low self-efficacy. According to a Harvard Business Review article, "At work, loneliness reduces task performance, limits creativity, and impairs other aspects of executive function such as reasoning and decision making."

There has been a lot of research over the past decade to help us understand just how important social connection is to our well-being. What's been most exciting for me to follow over the past five years is the growing understanding about how to build more meaningful connections at work and in life. At last, there is practical guidance and science-based tools that support the development of higher quality social connections—at work and in life.

How to Form More Meaningful Connections

So, what can we do to connect in more meaningful and satisfying ways at work? Social psychologist and researcher Dr. Julianne Holt-Lunstad identifies three major types of social support that can serve as a framework for strengthening our connections at work and outside of work.

- **Structural support**: size of relationship network; variety of relationships; frequency of contact
- **Functional support**: depth of interactions; feeling support is available
- **Quality support**: perceptions that interactions are positive

All three types of support inform the extent to which we feel high or low levels of social connection. At work, we may interact with a lot of people in our immediate physical or virtual work environment (structural support), but may not perceive that our coworkers care about our struggles, successes, or aspirations outside of our work responsibilities (functional support). If the first two elements are present, but we perceive our interactions to be largely negative (lack of quality support), this can also diminish our overall sense of connection at work and well-being.

Self-Reflection: Identifying the Social Support You Want

Consider the three types of support below. Reflect on the question prompts and then rate your satisfaction with each area as High, Medium, or Low.

Structural Support

> **Structural support** relates to the size of your network; variety of relationships; and frequency of contact.

Think about who you regularly interact with, particularly as part of your work. Perhaps there are people that you don't interact with as often as you'd like. You may have lost touch with people you used to feel a closer connection to as part of your work. Or you might have several really good friends at work.

How satisfied are you with structural support? (number/variety of relationships and frequency of contact)

o   High Satisfaction

o   Medium Satisfaction

o   Low Satisfaction

What stands out for you about how you would like to increase your satisfaction in this area?

Functional Support

> **Functional support** relates to the depth of interactions; feelings that support is available if needed.

Consider how supported you feel by your co-workers. Do you feel like you can count on them when you need mental, emotional, or tangible hands-on support? Perhaps there are barriers that get in the way of deeper conversations or maybe you feel like you have as much support as you desire.

How satisfied are you with functional support? (depth of interactions and feeling support is available to you if needed)

o   High Satisfaction

o   Medium Satisfaction

o   Low Satisfaction

What stands out for you about how you would like to increase your satisfaction in this area?

Quality Support

Quality support relates to perceptions about the positive or negative nature of interactions.

Consider your regular interactions with coworkers and how you would describe how they make you feel: positive, helpful, satisfying, included or excluded.

How satisfied are you with quality support? (perceptions about the positive or negative nature of interactions with others)

o   High Satisfaction

o   Medium Satisfaction

o   Low Satisfaction

What stands out to you about how you would like to increase your satisfaction in this area?

If you are feeling low satisfaction in one or more social connection areas, you are not alone in this! Researchers have been tracking declining levels of social connection globally. Read on to understand why social interactions do not necessarily lead to feelings of belonging.

An Epidemic of Loneliness

In 2023, the U.S. Surgeon General released an advisory calling attention to the growing epidemic of loneliness and named the workplace as one of many sectors with the potential to serve as a major source of social support. It makes sense, because full-time workers spend an estimated 2,080 hours a year interacting with others as part of their work. Even if you report to work in person every day, there is no guarantee you'll experience satisfying levels of social connection. Gallup researchers report that in 2024, one in five employees said they felt lonely at work. Another 2024 study found that in-person work interactions and working as part of a team were not linked to lower levels of loneliness. How can this be? The issue is that loneliness is not the same thing as a lack of interactions with others.

> *Loneliness is less about the physical state of being alone and more about a perceived gap between our desire for social connection and our actual experience of it.*

As I reflect on a time in my career when I felt the most disconnected from my coworkers, I realize I had strong levels of structural and quality support but lacked functional support. I believed that my coworkers valued my contributions, but I did not believe they cared about me as a person. Upon delving into the research on social connection and loneliness, I've come to understand that one root cause of loneliness is Imposter Syndrome.

How Imposter Syndrome Creates Isolation

In his 2020 book, *Leading with Character*, Dr. Jim Loehr distinguishes between performance character strengths, which are necessary for high achievement and performance, and moral character strengths, which reflect a value on how we treat others.

74

Performance character strengths include focus, persistence, confidence, and discipline, among others while *moral character strengths* include kindness, honesty, compassion, gratitude, and humility, among others. Performance character strengths contribute to high achievement regardless of moral character strengths. They drive focus on what is accomplished at the expense of how you accomplish it. In the example of my early performance review, I was overvaluing the destination and undervaluing the journey when it came to meeting work deliverables.

Loehr discusses Imposter Syndrome as one potential root cause of this imbalance, emphasizing performance over moral character strengths.

> **Imposter Syndrome** is the belief that one is inadequate or undeserving of one's role or success, leading to the belief that it's only a matter of time before others figure this out.

The fear of being exposed as a fraud feeds feelings of insecurity, causing one to work harder. Sacrifices are made along the way, and one can neglect self-care (e.g., getting rest, eating healthy foods, and fostering quality relationships). Most of us can relate to making tradeoffs between prioritizing work demands over self-care, but it becomes problematic when this occurs over a sustained period. Sometimes, we keep our guard up for good reason. If we reveal more of our authentic self to coworkers and it leads to lack of acceptance or feelings of rejection, it results in our reluctance to trust people. For this reason, it is best to choose one or two relationships where there is a foundation of trust already and expand your authenticity gradually, gaining confidence about how to do this.

It's worth the effort to build authenticity. According to Loehr, the self-doubt associated with Imposter Syndrome leads to a lack of trust and confidence in others, which makes them less likely to open-up and let others get to know them in a more authentic way. This can cause others to perceive those struggling with Imposter Syndrome as distant and unapproachable, which feeds a cycle of continued self-doubt and loneliness.

What I failed to realize early in my career is the vital importance of my relationships at work on my overall quality of life and well-being. As much as I tried to compartmentalize my life into the "professional me" and the "personal me," what was going on in my relationships at work carried over into my personal life. I kept my guard up and carefully protected and projected the image I wanted everyone to believe about who I was. Imposter Syndrome kept me from bringing my authentic self into my work, which negatively impacted my sense of connectedness and belonging.

There were other implications, too. To achieve results, my schedule was tightly packed with meetings, phone calls, and responding to emails. This did not leave time to join my coworkers for lunch or even for a 10-minute stroll around the building. One senior research associate started leaving articles on my chair about the dangers of sitting too long and the business case for taking breaks at work. It wasn't until I broke my jaw that I began to set new boundaries for how I used my time at work, including the number of meetings I accepted each day and how I approached my interactions with coworkers during those meetings.

Quality of Work Relationships Pays Off

Paying more attention to the quality of my work relationships paid off. I was more intentional about sharing about my personal life with others, and I invited my direct reports to do the same. This led to more genuine curiosity and people brought more of themselves into conversations. I noticed that meetings seemed less tedious and depleting, leaving me more energized.

As I got better at weaving elements of personal connection into my work conversations, other people noticed. On one collaborative research project, I received many positive comments from people about how much they enjoyed our phone conversations and my ability to build relationships, while also accomplishing project needs on the call. This way of conducting meetings became part of my new way of working.

The next set of reflections help to identify ways you can increase your levels of social connection as part of your work so you can reap these benefits.

Let's Explore: Improve Social Connection

Pick one or two relationships where you could intentionally try to increase levels of structural, functional, or quality support.

Consider setting up a standing meeting with this person or persons, even without a work-related agenda.

Identify those with whom you feel you are your most authentic. Then name two with whom you could be more authentic.

My most authentic relationships

1.

2.

3.

Relationships where I desire more authenticity

1.

2.

3.

What might be getting in the way of having more authentic relationships?

Developing More Authentic Conversations

Select one or two approaches below to weave into work conversations before or after talking about tasks and results.

- ☐ Engage in short (5-minute) informal chats that probe below surface-level concerns
- ☐ Schedule digital connection opportunities with peers that emphasize informal, personal conversations that are not task or work-related
- ☐ Incorporate small-group interactions/breakouts into larger gatherings or meetings
- ☐ Seek training for yourself and others to promote skill-building in the areas of psychological safety, authentic relating, forgiveness, and/or appreciative inquiry
- ☐ Add times for personal sharing into regular meetings or gatherings
- ☐ Incorporate relationship-building skills into professional development plans, including active listening, compassion, and emotional intelligence

Another way to support you in showing up more authentically in your life is to identify people who share your values, beliefs, or purpose. Identify the people in your life with whom you can share your purpose.

List others who may share your values or care about the same things you do.

Identify the people who may have a strong sense of purpose themselves and who might support you in living a life that aligns with your purpose.

What steps could you take to strengthen these relationships?

Improving Structural, Functional, and Quality Support

As I've reviewed the research on how to strengthen these three types of support, I've identified five practices that I've been testing in my life. These practices work!

Select one or more practices below to foster meaningful connection, and then turn to that page in this guide to complete the practice.

If it seems overwhelming to try all five of them, briefly skim through them and then select one practice to try in the next week. Come back to this guide and write down what worked and what didn't go as expected. Consider whether you want to try the practice again or move to a different one.

What to Expect

A practice might feel uncomfortable at first, and that's okay. These are named "practices" for a reason! Whenever we try something new, it is bound to feel a bit clunky. Think about the first time you tried a new sport or played a musical instrument. Give yourself grace and try the practice a few times before moving on. Think about each attempt as an experiment that helps you understand what works and what might require adjustment.

o **Practice 1**: Create Micro-Moments of Connection (MMOC) - *go to **page 80***
o **Practice 2**: Digital Communication Strategies - *go to **page 82***
o **Practice 3**: Identify and Deepen Work Connections - *go to **page 84***
o **Practice 4**: Active Listening and Authentic Relating - *go to **page 86***
o **Practice 5:** Express Empathy - *go to **page 88***

Practice 1: Create Micro-Moments of Connection (MMOC)

Researchers at the University of Michigan Center for Positive Organizations have been studying the behaviors that build higher quality connections in the workplace for decades. According to this research, not all connections are created equal. What we want is higher-quality connections. They have identified a set of practices that we can weave into brief moments of interaction with others. They call these "micro-moments of connection (MMOC)". These short interactions can "light us up" and leave us with a renewed sense of energy.

> **Micro-Moments of Connection (MMOC)** are brief, meaningful interactions that create significant emotional connections between people. These moments convey deep feelings and reinforce bonds through gestures, words, or actions.

Most of these practices take just a few seconds or a few minutes with focus on weaving them into the interactions we already have, such as a moment of eye contact, a few minutes of conversation about a fun weekend activity or important relationship, a shared challenge or celebration, expressing a bit of appreciation, a positive affirmation or remark, or a quick message to let someone know you are thinking about them.

Be intentional about looking for opportunities to create MMOC – at the start of meetings as people are gathering, during times of transition, whenever you are waiting for anything in the company of others, in casual interactions with text messages or the chat feature in a virtual meeting, or at the start of one-to-one calls.

To prepare for a one-on-one interaction, ask yourself, "What can I learn from this person? How can I support them? How can I show up as a human, sharing a little about myself instead of jumping right into tasks?"

Which MMOC practices would you be willing to try?

☐ Identify in advance how to show up as "more human"

☐ Make eye contact and keep coming back to it (naturally)

☐ Smile, wave, or shake hands to greet people

☐ Be fully present/pay attention

☐ Address people by name

☐ Use positive language (please, thank you, affirmations)

☐ Use positive body language (arms uncrossed, leaning forward, palms open)

☐ Focus on asking more, telling less

☐ Chat or ask about a fun weekend activity or event important to someone else

☐ Express gratitude or appreciation for something specific

Which of the MMOC practices feel most natural?

What steps will you take to make these moments happen?

How Did Your Practice Go?

If you tried the practice, how did it go? What might you try to do differently next time?

Practice 2: Digital Communication Strategies

Another area to consider is the influence of technology on our social connections. Think about this for a moment.

What are the different ways that you use technology to interact with your co-workers or with people as part of your work?

☐ Calendar

☐ Communication Apps (GroupMe®, WhatsApp®, etc.)

☐ Digital communication channels (Slack®, Teams®, etc.)

☐ Email

☐ Phone

☐ Social media posts

☐ Texts

☐ Video happy hours

☐ Video meetings

☐ Other

Clearly, there are a lot of ways that we use technology as part of our interactions at work. There are numerous ways that our use of technology can either help or hinder our social interactions.

When we become too focused on digital communication, it can replace time we might spend engaging with others in person. Technology tends to monopolize our attention when it is present.

Studies show that just having a phone out and present during a conversation interferes with your sense of connection to the other person, the feelings of closeness experienced, and the quality of the conversation.

How has technology influenced your ability to connect with others?

Has it negatively or positively impacted quality or frequency of your social connections?

How do you use technology to help you stay connected with people who matter most to you?

How can you be intentional in setting boundaries with technology when interacting with a colleague—whether in person or virtually?

How Did Your Practice Go?

If you tried to change use of technology in social interactions, how did it go? What might you try to do differently next time?

Practice 3: Identify and Deepen Work Connections

Identify at least one person at work whom you'd like to get to know better.

Reflect on the following prompts with this person in mind.

What do you already know about them?

What are you curious to learn more about them?

What do you already have in common with them?

Deepen the Connection

Use the responses on the previous page to brainstorm ways to deepen your connection.

How might you be intentional about improving your level of connection?

What actions can you take to deepen a connection in your work?

How Did Your Practice Go?

If you took action to deepen an existing connection, how did it go? What might you try to do differently next time?

Practice 4: Active Listening and Authentic Relating

We often listen with the intent to receive information or to find an opportunity to share what's on our mind. To improve connection, we may need to practice listening differently.

> **Active listening** is about intentionally listening to understand the other person's perspective, helping us connect to people in deeper ways that go beyond accomplishing the task at hand.

When conversations at work always revolve around work-related tasks, we miss the opportunities to connect more deeply with one another.

The key to deepening connections with others is to express an active interest in what they are saying and to help them feel heard. This set of practices identifies how to listen actively, offering suggestions for deeper conversations that feel more engaging and satisfying for the listener and the person being listened to.

Try using one or more active listening tactics to deepen understanding of another person's perspectives.

☐ *Summarize what you heard.* Some helpful ways to begin your response might be:
- What I hear you saying is...
- It sounds like...
- If I understand you correctly...

☐ *Ask questions that encourage deeper sharing.* Avoid jumping to conclusions about what you think they mean or feel. Instead, ask them!
- How did that make you feel?
- What happened next?
- What do you want to happen?

☐ *Use non-verbal body language that conveys interest.*
- Make eye contact if that is culturally appropriate.
- Nod.
- Face the other person.
- Maintain an open and relaxed body posture.

☐ *Avoid giving advice or problem solving* – at least right away. Make sure the other person's perspective is understood and that they are open to advice or ideas about how to respond.

Identify one active listening skill that you can bring into your next interaction:

o Summarize/paraphrase what you heard.

o Ask questions that encourage deeper sharing.

o Use non-verbal body language to convey interest (e.g., eye contact, nod head).

o Avoid giving advice.

o Avoid thinking about a rebuttal or your response while you listen.

How Did Your Practice Go?

If you took action to practice active listening, how did that go? What might you try to do differently next time?

Practice 5: Express Empathy

Learning to express empathy is important because it helps others feel heard and understood. Getting more comfortable expressing empathy can help us stay with conversations when someone shares something hard.

When we don't know how to respond, we might avoid deeper questions and connections. For example, we might not follow up and ask how a sick family member is doing or ask about a challenge someone is dealing with at work.

Empathy is the secret ingredient to making connections feel truly meaningful. Here are some of the benefits to showing empathy in your relationships.

- **Builds Trust and Rapport:** When people feel understood, they're more likely to trust others, leading to stronger, more genuine relationships.
- **Fosters Mutual Respect:** By showing empathy, we're acknowledging others' feelings and experiences, which promotes respect and a deeper sense of connection.
- **Enhances Communication:** Empathy helps us communicate more effectively by considering others' perspectives, leading to fewer misunderstandings and more productive interactions.
- **Supports Emotional Well-being:** When we empathize with others, we create a supportive environment where people feel valued and cared for, boosting their emotional health.
- **Encourages Collaboration:** In both personal and professional settings, empathy can lead to better teamwork and collaboration, as people are more willing to work together and support each other.

Empathy acts as the bridge that connects us on a deeper level, making our interactions more meaningful and impactful.

Techniques To Express Empathy and Build Stronger Relationships

These techniques often defuse emotionally charged situations. They help us to avoid responding reactively and help us to withhold judgment as we seek to understand.

- ☐ **Active Listening:** Give full attention to the person speaking. Maintain eye contact, nod, and use verbal cues like "I see" or "I understand" to show you're engaged.

- ☐ **Ask Open-Ended Questions:** Encourage deeper sharing by asking questions that require more than a yes or no answer. For example, "Can you tell me more about that?" "What happened after that?"

- ☐ **Validate Feelings:** Acknowledge and validate the other person's emotions by saying things like, "That sounds really tough," or "I can see why you'd feel that way."

- ☐ **Reflect Back:** Paraphrase what the person has said to show that you understand. For example, "So you're feeling frustrated because..."

- ☐ **Share Similar Experiences:** If appropriate, briefly share your own experiences to show you can relate. Focus on building a connection and direct attention back to their experience.

- ☐ **Show Compassion:** Offer support and understanding. Sometimes just saying, "I'm here for you," can mean a lot. Or, "I can see why you're upset about this."

- ☐ **Non-Verbal Cues:** Use body language and eye contact to convey empathy. Lean in slightly, keep an open posture, and show facial expressions that match the emotion being discussed.

- ☐ **Avoid Judgment:** It can be hard to hold back judgment or advice when we disagree with how someone has handled something or their perspective. Empathy focuses on understanding and supporting. Start there, and it might make others open to another way to approach a situation or to view it differently.

- ☐ **Be Patient:** Give the person time to express themselves without interrupting or rushing them to finish.

- ☐ **Offer Help:** If appropriate, offer to help or find a solution together. This shows that you're willing to support them actively. "What can I do to help?"

Can you think of a situation where empathy played a crucial role in deepening a relationship?

_____

_____

_____

_____

_____

_____

_____

_____

_____

How Did Your Practice Go?

If you practiced using empathy skills in a new conversation, how did that go? What felt hard about it?

Reflecting On Social Connection Practices

This section included a lot of practices. Every one of us has a different comfort level with these skills. Some might come more intuitively to you than to someone else.

Reflect on your overall takeaways before moving on. Check out the **Resources** section to go deeper on some of these skills.

Connection in Practice

Which of the practices did you try? Did your practice turn out as expected, above expectations?

What else would you like to do to continue to build deeper and more meaningful connections that support you in attaining your Ideal story?

CHAPTER 6

WAYPOINTS

- This chapter invited you to identify the relationships that matter most to you at work and in life.

- You reflected on the quantity and quality of your social connections and identified opportunities to strengthen them.

- You learned about 3 types of social support (structural, functional, and quality) and considered how satisfied you are with each area.

- You explored several practices that can help strengthen the three types of social support introduced in this chapter.

- The next chapter builds on social connection with others by introducing practices that help you to feel more connected to the world around you (transcendence).

Chapter 7

Transcendence

(Connect with Something Bigger than Yourself)

> "We may spend most of our waking hours advancing our own interests, but we all have the capacity to transcend self-interest and become simply part of a whole. It's not just a capacity; it's the portal to many of life's most cherished experiences."
>
> Jonathan Haidt, psychologist, researcher, professor, author

It's exactly 4:50 AM and I wake from a deep and restful sleep without an alarm. I close my eyes after a quick glance at the time and luxuriate in the quiet stillness as I get my bearings. What city am I in again? I can't honestly remember the name of it. It's more like a small mountain village than a city and we'll be moving onto the next town on the famed Camino de Santiago pilgrimage trail in a few hours. Being careful not to wake my husband, who is still asleep next to me, I slip out of bed and change into my yoga clothes.

As we were preparing for the rigors of this adventure across the Iberian Peninsula in Spain, I thought carefully about the grounding practices that I'd maintain during the trip. We hike from one town to the next, staying in different hotels every night. A travel service is taking care of the luggage and accommodation so we can focus our energy on being present and focused on the moments that unfold from sunrise to sundown as our small group of six makes its way down well-worn forest paths, through mountain villages, along highways, over rolling pastures, and across rivers and streams.

Preparing for the Unknown

We've trained for months to be able to complete 10 to 16 miles of hiking each day, so my morning yoga practice is not for the sake of a physical workout. The benefit is mostly mental. I've shortened my normal 90-minute Vinyasa flow routine to half that length, focusing more on the stretches and core strength moves. Moving through the familiar series of postures every morning allows me to check in with myself and mentally prepare for a day of unknowns. I am vaguely aware of the route we are taking, the key points of the terrain we'll be covering, the number of miles we'll walk to the next town, and what cultural or sacred sites we might encounter along the way. What's hard for me to anticipate is how I'll respond to the terrain, the weather, the conversations with others, or the lack of time alone. I normally work remotely most of the time, and it's challenging to be surrounded by people all day long. The tour guides take care of all the details and logistics, including the food placed in front of us at mealtimes. I'm beginning to realize that I'm more of a control freak than I'd like to admit.

As the yoga practice unfolds, I focus on my breath and let go of anxieties that surface about the day ahead. Even with the logistics of the day taken care of, there's plenty of mental chatter surfacing. I notice the chatter, name it, and let it go, returning to focus on my breath. I do the same routine everyday but somehow it feels different each day in my body and in my mind.

On the best days, my mind is still, and I sync my breath up with the flow of the postures, moving easily from one pose to the next. I'm 100% tuned into how it feels to move my body through space. I feel strong, vibrant, and energized. The minutes fly by and I savor the equanimity. Other mornings, my mind is so active that I need to keep a notebook and pen by my yoga mat because capturing thoughts on paper is the only thing keeping me from bolting from the mat to act on something that surfaces. I miss a cue from the yoga video on my phone and find myself in the middle of a pose that's supposed to come later. I tell myself to "be here now" or simply "focus."

As my yoga practice comes to an end, I savor one last deep breath before folding my travel yoga mat and nestling it into my suitcase. Within the hour, our travel group meets and exchanges "good mornings" over breakfast before check-out. We linger over freshly brewed coffee for a verbal review of the journey ahead, and then meet our guide and follow him down the sidewalk and over a bridge spanning a river. The chilly mountain air settles on the summer-warmed water, creating a dense layer of fog. I watch as the loud and boisterous group of hikers from Venezuela disappear into the mist on the other side of the bridge, thankful for the quiet serenity of the morning.

Transcending the Everyday

Our guide leads us across the bridge and onto the main trail. We fall into a steady rhythm, and I ground myself in the details of my surroundings. We marvel at intricately woven spider webs on shrubs alongside the trail and the beauty of the silky filaments that sparkle with drops of morning dew, belying the deadly work of art for the spider's unsuspecting prey. I again tune into my breath, notice the crunching of my boots on the trail and practice mindful presence. I seek to engage my senses, noting what I'm seeing, the feel of the moist fog on my face, the earthy smells of damp earth and pine needles. I feel a deep sense of connection to nature, to myself, to my small group of fellow travelers, to the millions of pilgrims who have gone before us in the thousand years since this pilgrimage trail emerged in the Middle Ages. This sense of connection to something bigger than myself is why I've come on this journey—to transcend daily concerns by the simple act of walking.

Self-Reflection: Experiencing Transcendence

Transcendence is a weighty term, and it can seem kind of mystical and "out there." The science in this area is fascinating! But, before I go there, let's consider if and how you might have experienced it in your own life. Research shows that most of us have experienced it.

Are there peak experiences that stand out in vivid technicolor in your memory? Perhaps moments of deep meaning or connection you find yourself returning to in your mind for healing, solace, inspiration, or challenge?

Are there times when you've felt a fullness of being that seemed to expand beyond you and at the same time to knit you together with nature or some element of creation?

Can you remember being at a concert or sporting event, surrounded by strangers and suddenly being swept up in a moment of pure joy or exhilaration because of what you saw happen on the stage or field?

I'll never forget the first time I saw the northern lights shimmering in the summer sky as a young child. I was with a good friend, and we were laying on our backs in the yard looking up at the night sky. The colors were particularly vivid, and we felt knitted together in the moment of being in the same place at the same time staring into the night sky.

The Meaning of Transcendence

Transcendence is a broad concept and there are aspects of it that overlap with our sense of purpose and our ability to feel connection with others. So, what does it mean?

> **Transcendence** means to rise above or go beyond our ordinary limits or everyday experience. It also means to connect with something bigger than yourself.

The connection to something bigger than yourself might be to nature, an idea, a community, a purpose, or to a deeper understanding of oneself. It might also feel like a greater connection to some aspect of the Divine. Research on transcendence focuses on measurable *transcendent mental states.*

> **Transcendent mental states** are specific psychological or emotional states in which a person feels they have moved beyond the ordinary experience of self or reality. Researchers often refer to these as "peak experiences."

Measurable transcendent mental states that show up in research include:

Awe	Inspiration	Gratitude
Consciousness	Joy	Love
Flow	Mindfulness	Wonder

What these states have in common is a blurring or weakening of the perceived boundaries between others, the world, and one's own self. And this blurring of separation results in increasing degrees of perceived unity.

> **Transcendent experiences** are the concrete moments or events that prompt a transcendent mental state.

Transcendent experiences are often brief moments of time but can be life altering, catalytic, and transformational. They are often perspective shifting moments, sparking new insights or a deeper understanding or appreciation of people or the world around us. They can be joyful, bittersweet, or painful. They are the experiences that sometimes break us wide open, marking a moment that indelibly divides our memories into "before" and "after." They can also be more subtle shifts in perspective that change how we view the world or interpret past events. Transcendent experiences can help us to show up as better versions of ourselves, feel more fulfilled in our lives, and support our well-being.

How Transcendence Fuels Well-Being

The mental states of awe, consciousness, flow, inspiration, joy, and wonder are powerful and transformative. As said before, they are also measurable. Researchers have been able to stimulate the emergence of these mental states and then observe what's happening in the bodies of those experiencing these states. Sometimes researchers will ask survey questions or ask study participants to journal about what they are experiencing or feeling. Sometimes they will observe what happens to the behavior of those they are studying for some time after the transcendent experience.

Most of the research on the benefits of transcendence focuses on what happens physically, mentally, and emotionally when we experience these mental states. Our brain chemistry and hormone levels change, our nervous system lights up in different ways, our immune function is bolstered, our inflammatory response is reduced, and there are positive changes in our cardiovascular system. These physiological and psychological pathways link self-transcendent mental states with increased helping behaviors, feeling more connected to others, higher levels of physical and mental energy, getting along better with others, less anxiety and depression, less loneliness, and higher levels of life satisfaction.

There are also benefits to our performance at work. Transcendent experiences transform our perspective including how we view ourselves, our context, and the world around us. We tend to be more open-minded and accept different points of view. Some studies suggest experiencing awe expands our perception of time, so we feel like we have more time available. This increases our ability to respond with more patience and generosity. In terms of relationships, we tend to be easier to get along with and more likely to help others.

All of this adds up to being more likely to show up at work, being more engaged and productive when we're at work, and finding more enjoyment and fulfillment in our work.

Who doesn't want more of these things?!

Consider the tangible benefits of experiencing transcendent states.
*Which of these benefits are you missing, or do you wish to see more of in your **Ideal** story?*

Fostering Transcendence

Transcendence can be experienced by individuals regardless of their affiliation with a religious or faith tradition. For example, many people experience transcendent mental states, in response to nature, a work of art, music, or a complex new idea. It might be the sense of awe that emerges when witnessing the miracle of new life or the connection to something bigger than us in the presence of the passing of a loved one or a brief look into a stranger's eyes.

For some, prayer can also be a gateway to transcendence, even for people who are not practicing it as an expression of religious belief. Casper ter Kuile, founder of Sacred Design Lab, describes the practice of prayer as ". . . being conscious... telling the truth... taking what has been unconscious and bringing it into open awareness." Prayer can be practiced alone or in the company of others; in a sacred space or in everyday mundane spaces; inaudibly (in silence) or audibly (through verbalizations, song, or chanting); and using a variety of postures (sitting, kneeling, standing, lying prostrate, or dancing).

Contemplative or introspective practices, such as journaling, yoga, and meditation, help us to be more attentive, intentional, and aware of our inner and outer world. They also help us to practice self-distancing or self-detachment, gaining a broader perspective of our circumstances, which helps foster consciousness. We may not experience transcendence while using contemplative practices, but with regular practice, they create conditions that foster self-transcendent mental states such as awe, joy, flow, and wonder. These moments may be fleeting, but they can elevate our emotions and mood states as well as transform our ways of thinking about and approaching the world in a positive way. The experience of transcendence is made more likely, and experienced more fully, when there is attention (presence), intention (directed toward something outside of ourselves), and awareness (perception of the world around us).

Self-Reflection: Creating the Conditions to Support Transcendence

Transcendence is more likely when we are able to just BE in the present moment, fully absorbed in whatever we are doing. Pause for a moment and consider the kinds of activities that fill you up, bring you joy, and activate your heart (inspire positive emotions). Are there things that allow you to let go of your worries, concerns, minor pains, or self-consciousness?

Circle what activities resonate most for you or add some of your own. Maybe add some details, like a specific setting, the type of activity or people who might be involved.

arranging flowers	listening to music
being in nature	looking at art
being in silence	making music
cooking or baking	meditation/reflection
creating something new	painting with watercolors
dancing by yourself	physical activity
dancing with others	playing a sport
enjoying a hobby	prayer
gardening	reading
interacting with animals/pet	singing
interacting with children	talking with friends/loved ones
journaling	volunteering/serving others
kayaking at the lake	writing

When was the last time you allowed yourself to engage in these activities?

Want to be more intentional about weaving these into your daily life? We'll explore this more in the final chapter.

Transcendent mental states cannot be manufactured—there are no guarantees here—but we can create the conditions to make them more likely. As I've combed through research studies on transcendent mental states, I've identified several strategies that can make these magical moments more likely. These practices inspire us to show up as our best selves and broaden our consciousness to respond more effectively to life's challenges. As I describe them in the pages that follow, consider which of these practices or strategies are most tangible and feasible for you.

Transcendence-Fostering Strategies

Consider adding one or more of these practices to incorporate into the flow of your work and life. Note that this might mean combining some of the activities you identified above with these strategies. Explore all of them in order or jump to a page that most interests you.

- **Practice 1**: Exposure to Nature – *go to **page 103***
- **Practice 2**: Presence – *go to **page 105***
- **Practice 3**: Minimize Distractions – *go to **page 107***
- **Practice 4**: Mindfulness – *go to **page 108***
- **Practice 5**: Volunteerism/Service – *go to **page 111***

Practice 1: Exposure to Nature

Experiencing nature is one of the most common ways to experience awe and wonder.

Which of the following are feasible ways to increase your exposure to nature?

- ☐ Increase exposure to natural light by sitting near a window
- ☐ Incorporate live plants or flowers into your workspace
- ☐ If live plants aren't an option, add realistic looking fake plants
- ☐ Post pictures of nature on walls
- ☐ Use screen savers with pictures of beautiful natural places
- ☐ Play natural sounds in the background such as birds, the sound of rain, or the ocean (wear headphones if you share a workspace)
- ☐ Step outdoors or open a window to feel the breeze on your face (wear a mask if air quality is a concern)
- ☐ Use a meditation app that includes scenes or sounds of nature

It's not enough for us to try to increase our nearness to nature. We've got to pay attention to experiencing it. Literally, stop to smell the roses!

In what ways might you pause to appreciate the beauty around you?

For example, when riding or driving, pay attention to the world passing by your window. Be intentional about noticing beauty in the landscape or the color of the sky or the shape of a cloud.

What opportunities are there to increase your exposure to nature in daily life?

How might you benefit from a brief walk or taking a break outside?

If you can't be outdoors, in what ways can you experience nature indoors?

For example, position yourself near a window for a five-minute standing break during daylight hours and pay attention to what you see outside. This can work in just a minute.

When you spend more time in nature, how does it make you feel?

Do you find it influences a shift in your thinking or in your mood or in how you behave?

Simply noticing what's going on in the world around us can be a powerful perspective shift, reminding us that what's going on inside the space in our head is small. We are on a big globe with around 8 billion other people each having their own moments, experiences, and challenges. Whatever ways you increase your exposure to nature, the next strategy is essential to it.

Practice 2: Presence

> **Presence** is a state of being fully engaged in what is happening in a given moment.

Presence is foundational for fostering transcendence. It's about focusing our attention on what's going on right here, right now. You may be surrounded by natural landscapes, artwork, or visually pleasing spaces. but the value to your well-being is lost if you don't have the capacity to pause and notice it. One of the foundational ways to foster transcendence is to create conditions that help focus attention and be more fully present. But it doesn't happen on its own. It takes intention and practice.

One of the simplest ways to start fostering presence is to **identify all the ways that you multitask throughout the day**. Multitasking happens whenever we are trying to do two or more things at the same time. For example,

> scrolling through your email while you are eating;
>
> watching television while you are working;
>
> sending a text to someone while you are talking to someone else.

Pay attention and list all the ways you multitask in one day.

Practice presence by identifying one common activity and focus your full attention on doing just that one thing.

For example, every day when you brush your teeth, focus your full attention on the task. Notice how you hold your toothbrush, how much pressure you are applying to your teeth, and if there are teeth that get less attention. Another opportunity might be to avoid multitasking when you are eating or snacking.

When could you practice being more present, for just a minute?

Reduce multitasking during breaks and rest periods too, which should be interspersed throughout the day. Do you automatically reach for your phone while waiting for something? Practice presence and mental awareness instead. Sitting quietly, stretching, or walking are other ways to incorporate mindful pauses into a hectic schedule.

> *Practicing presence can be very difficult in our hyper-networked digital world, where a single pause in the day often has us reaching for our mobile devices to check emails, updating our social media status, or checking out news headlines. A 2014 study found 67% of men and 25% of women were more likely to press a button to administer a shock to themselves rather than sitting quietly and thinking without distractions!*

Practice 3: Minimize Distractions

Minimizing distractions is a practice that can support our ability to be present. Perhaps you can identify with the deep satisfaction of being fully immersed in a task. Have you ever been so focused on something that you lost track of time?

> **Flow** is a state of deep engagement and focus, characterized by a sense of effortless action and complete immersion in an activity.

It is a transcendent mental state that is made more likely when minimizing distractions. Having a substantial uninterrupted stretch of time at work is increasingly rare. Some estimates say we are interrupted every eleven minutes while at work.

Suggestions for minimizing distractions are listed below. Identify the actions you could be more intentional about trying to incorporate into your daily life.

- ☐ Silence notifications from mobile apps, email, or social media or make them less disruptive on your devices.
- ☐ Create boundaries for how quickly you respond to non-urgent emails, text messages, and voice mail messages.
- ☐ Block your calendar for focused work, enabling automatic messaging that you will respond to all messages after a certain time.
- ☐ Install software onto your computer, or rely on features built into your smart phone, to temporarily mute notifications or disruptions.
- ☐ Create regular "office hours" when work colleagues are encouraged to reach out for questions or guidance. Discourage low-priority interruptions outside those hours.
- ☐ Move your phone to the other side of the room so you have to get up to look at it.
- ☐ Tidy up your workspace so you are not distracted by reminders, task lists, or other action items while working on a high-priority task.
- ☐ Turn away from your computer monitor or put your mobile phone out of sight to focus your attention during a meeting or conversation.

Select and experiment with one or two ideas in the next week.

Practice 4: Mindfulness

> **Mindfulness** is an intentional practice that includes letting go of judgment to become more aware of what's going on in our body or mind. It may include techniques like meditation, deep breathing, journaling, and body scans.

Mindfulness practices are intended to cultivate the state of being present. It is possible to be present without practicing mindfulness, but mindfulness strengthens your ability to remain present.

Of all the strategies associated with transcendent mental states, mindfulness might be one of the most well studied. Due to the link between mindfulness meditation and work performance, numerous organizations are implementing mindfulness training. A 2017 survey of US white-collar workers found one in six had participated in some form of mindfulness meditation practice in the past year.

Mindful Movement

When we think of mindfulness meditation, we often picture someone seated on a meditation cushion in a quiet space set apart from everything, but mindfulness can be integrated into the actions of your everyday life. If you are like me and fall asleep when doing seated meditation, I recommend trying **mindful movement** such as yoga, tai chi, or awe walks.

Awe walks are a growing interest covered in mainstream media. When going for an awe walk, don't multitask by taking a phone call or listening to music or a podcast. Instead, focus your attention on specific things around you. What are you seeing, hearing, smelling, and feeling? Notice the birds, the trees, the feel of sun or rain or wind on your face. Notice the smells of flowers or freshly mowed grass. Notice how your body feels to propel you forward. Any activity can be mindful if it's combined with focused awareness.

Side Trip!

If You'd Like to Spend a Little More Time Exploring

There are numerous free resources available to support mindfulness practices. See the **Resources** section for a list of mindfulness resources including a series of articles on awe walks.

Which of the following mindfulness practices or resources have you tried?

- ☐ Mindful movement (e.g., yoga, tai chi, chi gong, awe walks)
- ☐ Focused breathing exercises
- ☐ Guided meditation
- ☐ Visualization exercises
- ☐ Journaling
- ☐ Body scans
- ☐ Gratitude practice
- ☐ Mantra repetition (repeating a word or phrase)
- ☐ Other

What has your experience with these, or other mindfulness practices been?

What might be keeping you from exploring mindfulness further?

What one activity of daily life might you try to do more mindfully (with focused attention and intention)?

No matter the task you are doing, mindfulness can make it feel more meaningful or enjoyable. Another way to shift how we approach what we are doing is to orient ourselves to a **mindset of service.**

For example, I dislike folding laundry. Whenever I feel the dislike and irritation rise within me as I'm folding my family's laundry (because it seems like a never-ending chore), I try to shift my mindset to service. I think to myself what it would mean if this person were no longer a part of my life and how much I'd rather have this laundry to fold than to have this person removed from my life. This is where volunteerism and service come into play, which is our next set of transcendence-inspiring strategies.

Think about a necessary chore or task that you dislike.

How might a mindset of service contribute to something or someone that is connected to something bigger than the completion of the task itself?

Practice 5: Volunteerism/Service

Volunteerism helps us to connect to something bigger than ourselves as we work alongside others to address a common challenge.

Acts of service can help us to connect to others, deepening our sense of purpose, and connecting us to a cause. The research on volunteerism notes that well-being and transcendence is more likely to happen when people are truly volunteering, not being mandated to complete service. There has been so much research on how good volunteering can be for our mental health and emotional well-being that it can be tempting to pursue volunteer work for our own benefit. However, the positive benefits of volunteerism increase when people are doing something for the explicit purpose of helping others. It could be as part of a formal volunteer program or as a more general orientation to service as a lifestyle.

Informal acts of service happen when you do something that is kind or meets a need without it being required or asked of you.

Small daily acts of kindness might take the form of extending grace to someone who is rude or disrespectful towards you, such as allowing someone in a hurry to step in front of you at the grocery store, or picking up litter that you encounter while walking your dog.

At work, service might look like checking on a work colleague who is having a difficult week or volunteering to do an unpopular, but necessary, task for your team. There may be opportunities to volunteer at work or through a professional association. You could learn a skill that promotes well-being for others, such as completing mental health first aid training or learning CPR.

Throughout my career, I've looked for ways to contribute to the growth and development of my professional field of practice. I've served as a volunteer in professional associations, on advisory boards, and mentored students and younger professional peers. I practice taking care to accept only a manageable amount of volunteer work. Typically, I accept opportunities with a negotiated term limit and build in succession planning if I'm accepting a larger leadership role. This helps prevent me from overextending myself to the point where I am not protecting my own self care practices.

Which of the following volunteer or service practices have you tried?

☐ Formal volunteering for an organization in your community

☐ Formal volunteer role within the company you work for

☐ Informal acts of service in your community

☐ Informal acts of service in your company

☐ Informal acts of service at home

☐ Learn a skill that promotes well-being for others

☐ Intentionally mentor others in your field of practice

☐ Other

How do you currently practice volunteerism/ service in work or personal life?

How does volunteering or service currently align with your sense of purpose?

What groups or non-profit organizations exist in the area of your purpose?

What opportunities might there be to volunteer or coordinate a volunteer team event at work? Do you have a workplace volunteer/match benefit?

Let's Explore: How to Foster Transcendence

This chapter mentioned a lot of practices that might be new for you. I know from my own experience that when I am struggling with too much to do, it can feel overwhelming to be presented with a lot of new ideas at once. If that's what you are experiencing, take a deep breath.

It's okay to be aware of these practices without trying to adopt something new right now. Feel free to let go of anything that feels uncomfortable or not aligned with what is most important to you. If, on the other hand, you are curious and excited to learn more about these practices, check out the **Resources** section to go deeper.

Transcendence in Practice

Which of the practices in this section have you tried?

What did you experience in trying those practices?

Are there any practices you would like to learn more about to help you realize your Ideal story?

The next chapter aims to integrate the ideas and practices from all the chapters in this guide into a coherent plan that works for you. This is where we build a bridge between your **Current** and **Ideal** well-being stories.

CHAPTER 7

WAYPOINTS

- This chapter introduced the concept of transcendence: feeling connected to something bigger than yourself.

- You were invited to reflect on your experiences of transcendent mental states (e.g., awe, flow, joy, mindfulness, love, etc.), and identify the activities that make these states more likely.

- You explored five different practices that foster transcendent mental states and identified ways to build transcendence-fostering activities into your daily life.

- The next chapter invites you to revisit your **Current** well-being story and finish charting a course to your **Ideal** well-being story.

Chapter 8

Reimagine Your Story of Well-Being at Work

"Not only do we understand the world through stories, but we understand ourselves through stories. And the stories we tell about our lives become our lives."

Charles Vogl, author, advisor, educator

Starting with Well-Being in Mind

I am sitting in the airport in between flights when I see a text from my niece, Kiera. She's been reading her mom's copy of my 2022 book and wants my advice about how to prevent burnout as she considers moving from an hourly position to a corporate salaried role in a different company. I respond as soon as I receive the text message, asking when she might be free to chat. Within minutes she sends back, "Are you free to chat now?" Thankful for the long delay between flights, and the quiet corner in the airport, I put in my noise cancelling headphones and make the call. We briefly exchange greetings and then I jump straight into the reason for our call.

"Kiera, I'm happy you reached out to me. Can you give me some context and help me understand your concerns?"

"Sure thing. As you know, my current position is with a small family-owned business. It gives me a lot of creative freedom but there isn't much room for me to grow professionally. I've been exploring job openings with other organizations and put in an application for a corporate role that seems like it would give me more opportunities to develop and apply my creative skills. For some reason, I am feeling nervous about moving into a corporate environment, even though I know deep down it would be better for my career goals."

I'm listening with my eyes closed, focusing my attention to pick up cues and seek to understand her perspective before leaping into advice giving mode. "Again, thanks for reaching out to me, Kiera. Can you say more about what you are concerned about?"

A Desire to Begin Well

Kiera pauses for a moment as though considering her words and then confides, "It was your story of burnout in your book. I've seen how workplace stress has negatively impacted other family members in corporate jobs. I think my people-pleasing nature and passion for my work might put me at risk for burnout. I've had some managers who try to manipulate employees to try to increase productivity. It sucks! I know that if I am not careful to set boundaries as I grow in my responsibilities at work, that I could burn out faster than a box of matches. I've been protected in my current job by my hourly work status because they have to pay me for overtime. I'll lose that protection if I take a salaried role. Now that I'm a new mom, I am looking for advice on how to keep work and life in balance."

I can't help but experience a burst of pride in my niece's maturity. I feel honored that she's reached out to me for advice and consider what I might offer as she embarks on a major career change.

I think back to my own experience of seeking advice and support from my manager when I was experiencing burnout, and how frustrating it was to hear her say I had to figure it out on my own.

I reflect on the steps I took to set boundaries and expectations as I recovered from my injury and shared some of the lessons I learned the hard way, hoping to help her proactively identify ways of working that protect her well-being.

Tips for Balancing Work Ethic with Well-Being

- When you are talented and passionate about your work, it's natural to go above and beyond what's expected. This is especially true when you are starting a new role because it's natural to want to show people what you're capable of and test yourself with new challenges.

- In hindsight, I've learned that I can be my own worst enemy when it comes to establishing expectations for my productivity. As a former competitive athlete, I'm highly disciplined, self-motivated, and results oriented. I'm used to pushing the boundaries on my own capabilities. This can unintentionally contribute to expectations from coworkers (and myself) that I'll consistently deliver unsustainable levels of output.

- You are ultimately responsible for your own health and well-being. Organizations might offer some great programs and benefits, but people will accept as much as you give in pursuit of your work. Only you can decide how much you can give and still support your well-being.

- It's up to your manager to uphold company policies and support you in taking advantage of well-being programs and resources. This is more important than an organization saying it cares about employee well-being. I imagine the interview process will give you an opportunity to meet your potential supervisor. Come into that conversation with questions that help you understand that person's leadership style and expectations.

- Team dynamics are also important. How people communicate with and support one another has a direct impact on the well-being of each team member. Try to understand in advance what the team dynamics are. You could directly ask this of a potential manager or ask to talk to current team members. If you know someone who works in the organization, see if you can learn more about a specific leader or department you'd work with.

Kiera asks me some clarifying questions and agrees to reach out if she has additional questions. A few weeks later, she lets me know that she's accepted the corporate position. I congratulate her on the new job and can't help but ask how she navigated the conversations about employee well-being into the job interview process. These are the questions she asked the hiring manager, along with some of her thoughts about why she took the approach she did.

Questions to Ask a Hiring Manager

- How often do you have meetings with your employees?
- What is the team dynamic like?
- What is expected for work on weekends and outside of core hours?
- Are team events required outside of work hours or are these optional?
- How do you protect your employees from burnout?

These questions helped Kiera to learn that the hiring manager has experience supporting employees who are at risk of burnout. The hiring manager understands that creative insights often happen outside of core work hours and it's common for people to want to capture ideas or harness creative energy before they lose it. Kiera shares that as an artist, she's learned that "the muse is a strange mistress and sometimes working off the clock is a necessary evil to get a project done."

> *Self-awareness about how certain kinds of work might lead to overwork is critical to identifying strategies to support one's well-being and that of their coworkers.*

Kiera learned that the hiring manager is aware that overwork and stress leads to "crappy creative work" and is a detriment to productivity. To support employee well-being, the manager proactively checks in with each team member to monitor for overwork while balancing the need to meet project deadlines and foster strong team relationships. She learned that the team dynamic is casual and friendly. They enjoy chatting about hobbies and their personal lives, and the team "welcomes the weird" in other creative types.

These learnings from Kiera warm my heart because I really want the best for her. I love her fun, quirky sense of humor and delight in her silliness when she allows it to emerge. I sense she's feeling this opportunity would give her the opportunity to work more closely with other creative types and develop strong relationships (maybe even friendships) at work. I learn that her work would include being able to work with people in Asia, maybe even allow her to connect with her longstanding fascination with Japanese culture.

As she's preparing to transition to the new job, I ask her what steps she's planning to take to protect her well-being. I'm sharing Kiera's written responses to me in case they might inspire your own ideas about the strategies and tactics that you might consider for yourself.

Preparing to Transition to a New Job

- Establish strong boundaries for my working hours during the first two months. I know I need to demonstrate what I'm capable of but also want to be careful not to set unreasonable expectations for overwork.

- Establish guidelines for how to effectively work with the factory in Asia, understanding that the time zone difference requires I interact outside of my core work schedule.

- Ask my friends and family members to hold me accountable for patterns of work that seem to put me out of balance.

These are a solid set of guidelines that Kiera has created for herself as she embarks on a transition to a new job. Such times of transition are the perfect time to reflect on your own work life journey and consider making some adjustments. But we can also be more intentional about experimenting with small changes to our ways of working throughout our lives, not just during major job transitions.

Self-Reflection: Identifying What's No Longer Working

As you consider Kiera's desire to proactively protect and support her own well-being as she embarked on her career, what advice or lessons learned would you share based on your experience?

_____

_____

_____

_____

How have you created your own set of strategies and tactics or boundaries to support your well-being during times of challenge or high demand?

_____

_____

_____

_____

As you consider your Current well-being story, are there areas where you'd like to make some big or small edits?

_____

_____

_____

_____

One of the ways I started to experiment with new ways of working that better supported my health and well-being was by identifying **Replenishing Routines**. This section aims to help you identify, or create Replenishing Routines to try weaving into your life.

Replenishing Routines

When we think of living a healthy life, our thoughts might turn to health habits. **Replenishing Routines** are more than just habits. They have the power to transform everyday mundane moments into more meaningful moments. They draw upon the science of wisdom practices and rituals. Let's break this down with some definitions to help distinguish the difference.

Habits are *individual* practices that are performed consistently to the point of being automatic. They occur without much thought or intention.

Routines are a *sequence of practices* performed regularly to establish a consistent pattern, but they require some intention because daily life can disrupt the conditions necessary to trigger the automatic response of a habit.

Rituals are a *sequence of practices performed to create intention and meaning*. They are less focused on accomplishing a specific task and more about the emotions that surface while doing them. They can be grounding, calming, focus our attention, and prepare us to rise to the challenge of whatever is coming at us.

Replenishing Routines combine these ideas into a series of practices intentionally woven into the fabric of daily life to restore energy, support well-being and align with values. Replenishing Routines do not rely on willpower because the pleasure of doing them is its own reward.

Habit Versus Routine Versus Ritual

To help distinguish the difference, I'll use an example from my own life. I used to be an avid runner. Sometimes it felt great while I was doing the run, but as I got older, it felt harder on my body and less rewarding. Instead of changing to a different kind of physical activity, I relied on motivation and discipline to get me out of bed early, with my feet pounding the pavement before dawn.

There were a lot of things I enjoyed about being outside in nature and watching the sunrise, but the physical act of running became more and more of a chore. It became so uncomfortable for me to run that I started to dread it. Thus, began years of a love-hate relationship with running. It finally got to the point that when I had a severe ankle sprain that severed major ligaments in my ankle, I limped home and thought to myself, "Well, at least I can finally be done running." There were elements of **habit** and **routine** in my running, and perhaps a little bit of **ritual**. I created meaning that helped me to overcome the dread of the run.

Shifting a Routine to a Source of Replenishment

Fast forward to the present day and my daily yoga practice. I regularly get up at 4:30 or 5:00 AM so I have time for my full yoga practice before my first calls of the day. On days when I travel, I'll get up as early as 2:30 AM to get in a mini-practice. A friend recently told me that she admires my discipline, but I told her it has nothing to do with discipline or willpower.

I enjoy my yoga practice so much that I think of it as a gift that I give myself. On especially grueling travel or workdays, I have come to rely on my morning practice to help me show up feeling centered, grounded, and more mindful. It replenishes me rather than depleting me and helps me to show up as the best version of myself. That's what a Replenishing Routine is all about. Identifying what those are for you and weaving them into the fabric of daily life can fuel you to show up as the best version of yourself.

Harvard Business School professor Michael Norton shares the benefits of cultivating and regularly engaging in rituals in his book, *The Ritual Effect*. According to Norton's research, rituals have the power to serve as emotional catalysts that can energize, inspire, and elevate us. They can transform how we experience life and increase our satisfaction and enjoyment of life. They also help us to strengthen our connections with one another and help us to feel part of something bigger than ourselves. Rituals are a set of practices that can foster transcendence, and it's important to understand how they work because they can inform the creation of Replenishing Routines.

The Savoring Aspect of Rituals

There is a savoring aspect of rituals. If you've ever been to a restaurant with a sommelier, you've been exposed to the power of ritual. Master sommeliers have a deliberate process when it comes to tasting wine. There are special glasses, a specific way to pour wine, to examine the color, and they spend a lot of time swirling the glass and sniffing the aromas. Only then do they taste the wine and when they do, there are all sorts of acrobatics with the mouth and tongue to ensure the flavors of the wine can be fully appreciated. This attitude of savoring can be applied to the practices identified throughout this guide to support well-being through Replenishing Routines.

A Recipe for Creating Replenishing Routines

1. **Start by identifying a recurring moment** in your daily life.

   Is there a specific time, place, or occasion that you'd like to incorporate a Replenishing Routine? Consider replenishing routines that ground you as you begin your workday; energize you after a period of focused effort; help you to transition from a difficult meeting; prepare for the week ahead; bring closure to the end of the week; or make an unpleasant recurring task enjoyable or meaningful.

2. **Identify the intention** or what you hope to experience.

   Do you want to make a mundane task more fun? Enliven your commute? Make an activity you enjoy even more enjoyable? It's about finding ways to make meaning out of everyday actions.

3. **Identify a symbolic act** or special objects.
   It could be using a special mug for your coffee, lighting a candle as you soak in the tub, or a special lamp you turn on. Perhaps you seek to engage your senses by adding something to look at or touch or smell or taste or hear. Maybe it's music, a special kind of food, or a favorite beverage.

4. **Create a narrative** by bringing these elements together in a sequence of events.
   Think about how it will begin, what happens in the middle, and how you want to close the replenishing routine. What type of behaviors or actions can help you to pay attention to the present moment and savor an experience?

Replenishing Routines bring together the practices you select from this guide and organize them into regular behavior patterns that transform perspective, thinking, how you experience your world, and how you respond within it. This journey of transforming leads to living out your **Ideal** story.

Let's Explore: Weave Replenishing Routines into Your Rhythms of Life

Reflect on Your **Current** story.

What Replenishing Routines exist in your life now? Which ones would you like to maintain or increase?

What well-being practices would you like to turn into Replenishing Routines?

Use the steps below to create a Replenishing Routine. An example is provided to illustrate the steps.

Example

Selected Practice: Wind down before bedtime.

1. *Identify a recurring moment or event in your schedule.*

   - *30 minutes before bedtime.*

2. *Identify the intention you'd like to bring into that moment or event.*

   - *Process the events of the day and let go of concerns that might keep me from sleeping.*
   - *Self sooth without eating "comfort food" or watching tv.*

3. *Identify symbols, actions, or objects and incorporate the senses (sight, sound, smell, touch, taste).*

   - *Special mug with my favorite chamomile tea, my leather journal, favorite spot on the couch.*

4. *Create the narrative (flow of events/actions).*

   - *Start to brew tea 45 minutes before bedtime.*
   - *Turn on soothing music without lyrics, volume turned low.*
   - *Dim the lights so they are not bright, but with light to write.*
   - *Take first sips of tea and savor the smell and taste.*
   - *Open my journal and process the highs and lows of my day.*
   - *Identify what concerns me and state my hopes for how things will turn out.*
   - *Sip my tea, savoring the chance to be still, not taking action.*
   - *Identify what I'm most grateful for and what I am looking forward to tomorrow.*
   - *Set an intention for how I want my day to go tomorrow.*
   - *Close journal.*
   - *Finish my tea and take a deep breath.*

Your Replenishing Routine

Selected Practice:

1. **Identify a recurring moment** or event in your schedule

   -

2. **Identify the intention** you'd like to bring into that moment or event.

   -

   -

3. **Identify symbols**, actions, or objects and incorporate the senses (sight, sound, smell, touch, taste).

   -

4. **Create the narrative** (flow of events/actions).

   -

   -

   -

   -

   -

   -

   -

   -

   -

Tips for Adding Replenishing Routines

Add only one Replenishing Routine at a time to allow time for you to adjust to the flow and develop a response to disruptions. If you fall out of a new Replenishing Routine for some reason, simply make an intention to begin again with a new starting time and day, then "show up" by practicing the routine at the next established trigger point. Extend yourself a good amount of grace and experiment as you adapt these routines. Over time, they will become a meaningful part of living your **Ideal** story.

Replenishing Routines are one way to foster more meaning, enjoyment, and fulfillment in your daily life. You may incorporate them into work tasks, into your commute, or in the transitions between home and work environments.

What next steps are stirring within you? How do you feel called to make a positive difference in your own life and in the lives of others by applying this information to your own life?

The path lays before you and it is up to you to begin writing the next chapter of your **Ideal** story. The final section of this chapter aims to integrate the work you've done up to this point into some specific changes to how you think about and approach the way you work.

Let's Explore: Current Story to Ideal Story

In this section, we'll bring forward all of the actions and thinking you've noted to put it all together as a personal roadmap from **Current** Story to **Ideal** Story.

Revisit your Current well-being story from page 21.

*This represents how you show up today in support of your roles, responsibilities, and highest priorities. Based on the reflections throughout the guide, what more would you add? Briefly restate the aspects of your **Current** well-being story most important to you.*

Revisit your Ideal well-being story from pages 24 and 45.

This is what helps you understand how you wish to show up as the best version of yourself. Summarize your thinking: Who do you wish to be and for what purpose? Are there certain relationships you want to develop or prioritize?

Revisit your Actions.

*Review page 45 and chapters 5-7 of this guide to identify the priorities and Practices you flagged in the **Let's Explore** sections throughout. This list gets them all in one place:*

☐

☐

☐

☐

☐

☐

☐

☐

☐

☐

☐

☐

☐

☐

☐

☐

Organize the Practices above by marking them according to each dimension below. Consider which area seems to present the biggest opportunity for you right now. Which area could be the most significant focus as you begin to create your **Ideal** story?

_ *P*   **Purpose:** Connection to purpose and values

_ *C*   **Connection:** Connection to others, including coworkers

_ *T.*   **Transcendence:** Connection to something bigger than myself

Rank your P, C, T list and identify the **top three Practices** that are most important to your **Ideal** story here:

1.

2.

3.

Add support partners.

*Who might support you in your journey towards creating your **Ideal** story?*

Create a visual side-by-side comparison: Current story to Ideal story

*Revisit the answers to your assessment on pages **22-23** and your reflections throughout.*

- List the positive contributors to your **Current** state of well-being on the left.
- List the positive contributors you wish to make part of your **Ideal** story on the right.

An example is included on the next page.

Example Side-by-Side Comparison

Current Well-Being Practices	Ideal Well-Being Practices
Annual wellness visit, labs & biometric screening	*Annual check in with my purpose and values. Establish intentions for how I want to BE instead of new year's resolutions*
Daily food tracking and exercise journaling	*Journal 3 Gratitudes each evening*
Minimum 7 hours of sleep	*15-minute replenish routine before bed for better sleep*
Run 3 days per week	*10-min mindful yoga after running*
Respond to emails during breaks	*Use Calm app for 5 minutes during afternoon break*
Watch television after dinner each night	*One night a week, break out my water color pencils & draw*

Your Side-By-Side Comparison

Current Well-Being Practices	Ideal Well-Being Practices

Create a Plan for Top Three Actions

What gets tracked and planned often gets done. Organizing a plan takes intention a step further. Don't worry about adding all your ideas into your plan at one time. Focus on what is most feasible or important right now. You can always revisit this list later and shift to different practices. Consider blocking time on your calendar to remind you of the actions you plan to take.

Sample Plan

Dimension	Action	Timing	Ideal Story Outcome
Purpose	Identify words, images, phrases that represent what matters most to me in life	This month	Use of my time and energy is aligned with what matters most. I am able to let go of commitments that don't align with what matters most.
Connection	Schedule walking call or in person walk to reconnect with 2 friends I have not seen in awhile	Reach out to friends this week to schedule time next month	I feel more in touch with what's going on in my friends' lives; we better support one another.
Transcendence	Buy a new sketchpad and dig out my water color pencils. Protect one hour each Thursday evening to draw.	In two weeks	I am feeling more joyful and fulfilled by reconnecting to my art.

Your Plan

Dimension	Action	Timing	Ideal Story Outcome
Purpose			
Connection			
Transcendence			

Make it Visual: A Vision Board for Your Ideal Story

Life gets busy and it can be hard to remember the intentions that we set for ourselves. When it might take some time to realize your **Ideal** story, it can help to visualize what it will look like to see if fully realized.

> A **vision board** is one way to help you visualize your Ideal Story. It might include words, images of actions you want to take, or the symbolic results of those actions, like peacefulness.

How to Create a Vision Board

1. Review your **Ideal** story.

2. Group common/similar ideas together like categories.

3. Identify images, words, or symbols that represent the **Ideal** story. Similar items can use the same images or words. Place them near each other on the board.

4. Create your board. Use colors and materials that are most pleasing to you.

5. Display your vision board in a place you'll see it often or take a photo and save it as your screen saver.

6. Update your board periodically.

7. Consider doing this activity with family, a friend group, or a work team.

Closing Thoughts

When you pick up a new book and consider whether you will read it, what informs you of your decision to buy it and invest the time? Perhaps you picked up this book because you are hungry for change. Or maybe it's part of a class you are enrolled in.

I've opened each chapter of this book with my own personal story about how work has been a positive or a challenging influence on my well-being. I had a wake-up call that signaled to me I needed to create a new way of working for the sake of my health and well-being. Telling my story illustrates what it might look like to pursue a whole person approach to well-being. Every individual's path will be different. There are likely some pieces of my journey that resonate with you and many that don't.

Activities and practices throughout this guide have invited you to consider trying practices that might not be part of your life today. This guide is an invitation to edit or rewrite the next chapter of your story. What is the story of transformation that you'd most like to tell in the future? Would you like to make a date with yourself to check in on what you wrote in this guide, identify what you have achieved, and if there are new practices you want to explore?

It can be powerful to share our stories with others. Are there people in your life who you could share your story with or who might enjoy trying some of the new practices with you?

Sharing our stories with one another can be a pathway to stronger, more genuine connections, breaking down barriers, helping us to develop empathy for one another, and contributing to our own physical, mental, and emotional well-being. As we collectively share our unfolding stories, we can co-create a new shared story about what it means to experience deeper purpose, richer connections, and transcendent moments within the world of our work.

CHAPTER 8

WAYPOINTS

- This chapter shared a case study and examples to proactively create a way of working that protects and supports well-being.

- You were invited to reflect on your **Current** well-being story and identify how you might create your own set of strategies to better support your well-being.

- You learned about Replenishing Routines and identified some ways of weaving well-being practices into your daily life.

- You revisited the practices from chapters 5 – 7 and identified the top practices that might support your **Ideal** well-being story.

- Your created a plan to incorporate the top practices into your life and created a vision for your **Ideal** well-being story.

You're nearing the end of this guide and you have a starting point for a new way forward. You'll likely encounter some storms and challenges as you navigate your way towards your **Ideal** story.

This is an invitation to experiment with the ideas and practices throughout the guide. If something doesn't seem to be working, reflect on what feels challenging about it. Trust that the practices will feel stronger and more comfortable over time. That's why they are called "practices"!

Keep reading to learn how some of these practices supported me when I experienced a significant threat to my well-being and what I discovered as I worked my way through that challenge.

Epilogue
Maintaining an Even Keel

It's been 15 years since my "wake-up" moment. Since that time, I've experimented with a number of practices, many of them mentioned in this book. Some of them worked, some of them back-fired and wore me out or created new compulsions. Other practices were wonderful and got me where I wanted to go, for a season. And still others became part of my new routines. I wasn't aware of how powerful these practices were until I found myself in the midst of another health crisis.

An Unexpected Detour

I've always had a weak ankle, with countless ankle sprains since my high school track days. In 2015, I turned it so badly, that I did 6 months of physical therapy and decided to stop running. In 2021, I had another major ankle sprain during my last training hike for the Camino de Santiago pilgrimage during my sabbatical. I recovered enough to complete the hike with an ankle brace, ankle-high hiking boots, hiking poles, and the strategic use of Ibuprofen and ice. Sometime after I returned from the hike, I went to see an ankle specialist because I could no longer bear weight without pain. The MRI and X-ray images confirmed that I'd totally severed two of the major ligaments in the ankle joint and I had a lot of arthritis and bone fragments in the joint. If I didn't have surgery, I would keep spraining the ankle.

After getting a second opinion confirming the diagnosis and recommended treatment, I booked the surgery and started to clear my calendar for the two months I'd need to recover and go through physical therapy. The surgery went very well and after six weeks, I thought the worst was behind me. Things took a dramatic turn the night before I was scheduled to visit my ankle surgeon for the follow-up visit that I thought would end my need for a walking boot and crutches. My ankle started to swell, and I felt nauseous. I went to bed hoping it was a mild case of the flu that was going around.

Shipwrecked!

By the next morning, the ankle had swollen substantially, the skin around the ankle was bright red and hot to the touch. I was in a lot of pain. I had my husband take me directly to the Emergency Room where they confirmed I was in a state of sepsis. I'd done so much to maintain my well-being practices, and we were at a loss to understand what had derailed my healing process.

The ER physician called the surgeon who had performed the initial ankle surgery and arranged to have me transported to the hospital where he met me to reopen the incision and flush the joint of the infection. The surgery seemed to go well, and I was placed in post-operative care overnight for observation. Our relief was temporary. In the middle of the night, my husband was contacted with news that I was in intensive care with pneumonia and my kidneys were shutting down. He drove back to the hospital to find me in the ICU with no less than eight tubes, wires, and sensors connected to my body. I was in ICU for a week, trying to make sense out of what had happened. There were at least fourteen specialists working with me, and I found it hard to keep track of who was visiting me throughout the day. After seven days, I was stable enough to be moved out of ICU but was still on oxygen and had a hard time taking a deep breath.

Replenishing Routines for Healing

After a full week of lying in a hospital bed, and with no idea how long I'd be there, I decided to try to incorporate some of my spiritual practices into a bit of a routine. I asked my husband to bring my journal, phone, and headphones to the hospital the next day when he came to visit.

For the next week or so, I woke up each morning well before dawn when the nurses came to do my daily blood draw. It was the start of a long day of disruptions with nurses monitoring my vitals every few hours, meal trays being delivered and removed, and a series of visits from the various doctors and specialists working on my case. In between, there was a lot of down time alone in my room.

Replenishing Routine 1: Mindful Movement

I created a mini yoga practice in my hospital bed. It was nothing more than 15 minutes of breathwork and gentle stretches, but it felt good to move my torso and do some mind-body movement. With each breath I visualized the air pushing the fluid out of my lungs.

Replenishing Routine 2: Journaling

After yoga, I journaled. I started with updates on my physical health status based on how I was feeling and the test results that were reported back to me by the nurses and doctors. Then a mental scan of how I was doing mentally and emotionally. I catalogued the many points of gratitude for small things like attentive care from my nurses, encouraging texts from friends, and the daily visits with my husband.

Replenishing Routine 3: Guided Meditation

I wrote prayers for healing and discernment for the doctors about the best course of treatment. I didn't have the energy to read or the interest to watch tv, so I played a series of guided meditations for post-surgical healing that a friend had recommended to me before my first ankle surgery. These became grounding practices that sustained me while in the hospital.

Replenishing Routine 4: Prayer

At some point I downloaded a health-care app that allowed me to gain access to my medical records, test results, and communications with my doctors. I accepted the option to allow a daily prayer notification from the app and found the prayers so encouraging that I started to screen capture them and download them to my computer for future reference. I eventually printed out many of my favorite prayers and put them in my journal for easy reference.

Replenishing Routine 5: Connecting to Others

I enjoyed several surprise visits from professional peers who had heard about my confinement when I posted to social media about needing to cancel several speaking appearances. Due to complications from the infection, I was on disability for another four months and had to cancel numerous additional in-person and virtual speaking engagements. I'm especially thankful for the professional peers who stepped into speaking commitments that I couldn't honor when my doctor prohibited me from travel. The follow-up care I required after I was released home was rigorous enough to require the help of a weekly visit from an in-home nurse and the arrival of my twin sister, who came to support my husband in providing the daily care that I required. Severe anemia sapped my energy, and I had no less than seven health-care appointments a week. But I was thankful to be surrounded by the comforts of home and the attentive care from family members.

Replenishing Routine 6: Nature

After two weeks in the hospital, I savored the sight of the flowers and hummingbirds in my backyard as I rested on the couch in my living room. My sister noticed how even a few minutes of time outdoors uplifted my mood and she made a point to help me get outside each day.

Throughout it all, I maintained a series of spiritual practices that included prayer, meditation, journaling, gratitude, yoga, social connection, and time in nature. They didn't change the circumstances I faced but they supported me through moments of pain and frustration that I simply had to journey through.

Reengaging Routines

As my strength returned, I began to reengage with friends, mostly virtually but eventually in person. I was touched when one of my professional peers surprised me with a plant that she'd been nurturing for months, thinking of me every time she watered it, sending healing thoughts. She also dedicated her morning meditation practice to me for many months. It means the world to me that there are people who care about me enough to do such things. It's particularly meaningful as I think back to how much I once struggled to turn professional relationships at work into genuine friendships.

As much progress as I've made in the past 15 years, I still consider my journey to be a work in progress. I'm thankful to have meaningful work and the energy to get out of bed before dawn most days to engage in the spiritual practices that I've come to call "Temple Time." I reflect nearly daily on my purpose and carefully weigh my commitments to maintain my well-being. Even so, I struggle with the tendency to overwork. Over the past year, I've found myself reverting back to my old habits of getting back on my laptop to answer email or to work on projects after dinner. I struggle to maintain monthly catch-up calls with my best girlfriends and notice that some "fill me up" activities have taken a back seat to work. That's when I have to reset my boundaries and reclaim my non-working time. It's a nearly constant struggle, so I don't think I'll ever feel like I've "arrived" at the destination of whole person well-being.

Tiding Over

Well-being is like the ebb and flow of the tide. It has natural highs and lows; change is inevitable and necessary. Successfully navigating with the tides requires patience, presence, and intention. Likewise, the well-being journey requires us to learn to listen to the rhythms of our own inner tide.

I find myself reluctant to schedule things too far out in advance, wanting to be certain that I'm heading in the right direction before I continue. It's a balance of sailing and tiding over. It accepts changes in the wind, unexpected squalls, choppy waves, and the placid glass of doldrums. I chart my course then navigate the conditions with greater presence and patience to get there.

About the Authors

Jessica Grossmeier

Jessica Grossmeier, PhD, MPH is an award-winning researcher, speaker, and author of *Reimagining Workplace Well-Being: Fostering a Culture of Purpose, Connection and Transcendence*. As a leading authority in workforce well-being, she was recognized as "one of the most influential women leaders in health promotion" by the *American Journal of Health Promotion*. Dr. Grossmeier collaborates with employers and well-being service providers to identify and apply best practice approaches to individual and organizational thriving. For more information about Jessica, visit her website at https://JessicaGrossmeier.com/About.

Rhea Fix

Rhea Fix, MEd, SPHR, is a strategic leader and instructional designer with more than 20 years of experience in learning and organizational development. As a consultant, she has developed and facilitated programs for Fortune 500 organizations, non-profits, and learning companies. She has developed award-winning programs and is published in industry journals. Her contributions to other books and journals in the learning industry span decades. For more information about Rhea, visit her profile at https://www.linkedin.com/in/rheafix/.

Resources

The resources below are a partial list of science-based resources, trainings, and tools that support individual well-being. It's always a risk to share web-based resources because the URLs can change and sometimes organizations shift ownership of their content to other entities. At the time of publication, the following resources were available through the organizations and links as listed. Additional resources are available at https://JessicaGrossmeier.com/Resources.

Chapter 2
Harvard Flourishing Index *and **The Flourishing App:*** by Human Flourishing Program at Harvard University's Institute for Quantitative Social Science.
- Twelve activities grouped into 4 categories, in alignment with the six domains of flourishing measured by the Harvard Flourishing Index.
- Web-based resources: https://flourishing.app/

Chapter 4
Mental Health America is the nation's leading national nonprofit dedicated to the promotion of mental health, well-being, and prevention.
- Gain access to resources, assessment tools, and local mental health support
- Topics include burnout, loneliness, depression, anxiety, neurodiversity, sleep, and eating disorders
- Web-based resource: https://mhanational.org/get-help

Chapter 5
Values Assessment Tools by Values Institute
- Guidance on the importance of values assessment tools and research on their effectiveness
- List of free values assessments currently available

- Values App Assessment by the Values Institute
- Web-based resource: https://values.institute/a-guide-to-free-values-assessments/

Finding Purpose and Meaning in Life: Living for What Matters Most by Dr. Victor J. Strecher
- Free online course on Coursera with four modules
- Self-directed course with approximately eleven hours of content
- Web-based resource: https://www.coursera.org/learn/finding-purpose-and-meaning-in-life

Purpose Development Tools by Dr. Zach Mercurio
- Interactive tools to explore and define your sense of purpose
- Web-based resource: https://www.zachmercurio.com/tools/

Chapter 6

Greater Good Science Center at UC Berkeley
- Publishes *Greater Good Magazine* to share practical guidance on mindfulness, purpose, social connection, workplace well-being, stress management, and many related topics
- Online courses, blog articles, seminars, and other resources make the science of meaningful life accessible and practical to the general public
- Web-based resources: https://greatergood.berkeley.edu/key

Social Connection Tools by U.S. Department of Health and Human Services
- Framework for a national strategy to advance social connection, including how to create a culture of connection at work
- Curated list of resources by other agencies and organizations to promote social wellness and reduce loneliness
- Web-based resource: https://www.hhs.gov/surgeongeneral/reports-and-publications/connection/index.html

Chapter 7
Mindfulness & Meditation Resources by Stanford Health Care
- Series of audio meditations to promote sleep, relaxation, pain management, relieve stress or anxiety, coping with grief, etc.
- Mindfulness resources by University of California organizations
- Web-based resource: https://healthlibrary.stanford.edu/books-resources/mindfulness-meditation.html

Free Mindfulness Project
- Mindfulness resources based on mindfulness-based stress reduction, mindfulness-based cognitive therapy, and other related approaches
- Audio mindfulness exercises, mindful breathing practices, body scan meditations, guided imagery, and many other tools
- Web-based resource: https://www.freemindfulness.org/

Awe Walk Articles by the *New York Times*
- "An Awe Walk Might Do Wonders for Your Well-being" by Gretchen Reynolds. September 30, 2020
- See the article: https://www.nytimes.com/2020/09/30/well/move/an-awe-walk-might-do-wonders-for-your-well-being.html
- "This Kind of Walk Is Much More Than a Workout" by Jancee Dunn. June 2, 2023
- See the article: https://www.nytimes.com/2023/06/02/well/move/walking-workout-awe-mental-health.html

Epilogue
- Guided meditations to promote successful recovery from surgery
- https://healthlibrary.stanford.edu/books-resources/mindfulness-meditation.html

Acknowledgements

As I was writing "Reimagining Workplace Well-being" in 2021, I wasn't sure what its impact would be. I hoped it would inspire those doing the hard work of developing and implementing workplace well-being initiatives to broaden their approach to include spiritual elements. Typically, workplace well-being has been the responsibility of professionals in the Human Resources, Benefits, Employee Assistance, or Occupational Health and Safety departments in an organization. So, I was surprised when I learned that people were buying copies of the book and sharing it with friends and family members who were not representative of my intended audience. Later I started receiving invitations from colleges and universities to help translate the highly conceptual content into more practical guidance for individuals interested in a whole person approach to well-being.

At first, I resisted the call to meet individual needs. After 20 years as a researcher, I was more comfortable educating around the systemic and strategic approaches to advancing population health. For the past 10 years, most of my research has not focused on evaluating individual behavior change interventions. I am deeply grateful to Stanford University for allowing me to test the earliest versions of the practices and processes captured in this guide with their Healthy Living community. An extra special thanks to Dominique Del Chiaro and Carol Hunter for coming alongside me as Zoom co-pilots through numerous iterations of the content, which relied on evolving technology.

Other institutions of higher education followed, including Case Western Reserve University, George Mason University, and UC-Berkeley Haas School of Business. What shocked me most was the day I received a call from Derek Bell about his use of my book for his MBA students at UW-Stevens Point. Based on positive feedback from his students, he incorporated the book as a core element in his curriculum. This news is what prompted me to consider creating a workbook that would help individuals apply the content from the first book into their personal well-being journey.

There is a Sufi proverb that says, "If you want to go fast, go alone. If you want to go far, go together." It beautifully represents the Sufi emphasis on community, collaboration, and the long-term benefits of shared journeys, especially on a spiritual path. I could not have wished for a more perfect companion for this writing adventure than my twin sister, Rhea Fix. Her academic training and experience in adult learning and instructional design made her the ideal collaborator for this work. I'm so thankful for her patience as the process unfolded in sometimes unexpected directions and for her encouragement when the calling felt challenging to me. We passed the manuscript back and forth, and it was amazing to see how much order she managed to create, wrestling my wandering feet back to the throughline we'd discussed during our weekly calls. Words fail to express how much admiration and respect I have for Rhea. Always game for a new adventure, she was immediately on board when we started to play around with the metaphor of "charting your course" on a journey. Having completed boat captain certification last Summer, all use of boating terms is attributed to her. It was a dream come true to collaborate on this project and I'm already anticipating the next great "adventure of Spunk and Zip."

Even though I was in great hands with Rhea as a collaborator, I am thankful to have again called upon my friends and professional peers to serve as pre-readers for the manuscript. I'm grateful for every single one of you who made time to review and provide substantive feedback on the early drafts. Thank you: Kathy Meacham Webb, Suzy Harrington, Patty de Vries, Brian Hughes, Alexandra Donovan, Jack Bastable, Lexie Dendrinelis, MJ Shaar, Abigail Barth, Susan Bailey, Samantha Tremlin, Derek Bell, Laura Putnam, and Keely Goss. A special thanks to Sean Foy and Dee Eastman for sharing their use of the term "Replenishing Routine" for restorative rituals, and for inspiring me to explore faith-based well-being through *The Daniel Plan*.

Thanks also to Teresa Malone, for her editing support and honest feedback. Collectively you provided encouragement, enthusiasm, insights, and critical commentary that elevated the quality of this guide far beyond my initial drafts. This is the work of transcendence! You were part of something bigger than any one of us and I'm so very glad for your involvement.

I am also deeply thankful for the many researchers whose work has informed my writing and thinking about this subject matter. The end notes scarcely do justice to the many years of devoted scholarship represented in the books, studies, and published works by those listed. Special thanks to Scott Barry Kaufman for the masterpiece, *Transcend: The New Science of Self Actualization*. The very act of reading the book was in and of itself a transcendent experience.

As I started working on this guide, I relied on a writing process and framework that I learned while writing my first book under the stellar guidance of Catherine Gregory and Nathan Joblin at Modern Wisdom Press. The process served me well and I am thankful for their continued support of my work, even though I chose to try self-publishing this time around. I continue to recommend them to anyone attempting their first book.

Any writer will attest the most challenging obstacle to getting a book written is making the time to sit in the "writing cave" and slog the cursor across the white space on the digital page. I am eternally thankful to the family and friends who were patient and understanding when I needed to preserve "off-the-grid" writing time.

Whenever I set my sights on a new adventure, my provisioning and planning includes checking in with my partner in life, Christopher Grossmeier. This guide opens and closes with stories that feature his seemingly boundless care, love, and support. No matter what I'm doing, where I'm headed, or how tricky the terrain, he remains an essential steadying force that allows me to push myself out of my comfort zone. Thanks for your endless encouragement and support to follow the calling into the fog. Love of my life for nearly forty years, you are the home base I long to return to.

And finally, I must acknowledge the Source of all that is created.

Thank you for the gifts of strength, inspiration, and margin in my schedule to complete this work. Thank you for the gift of meaningful work. I commit this artifact to Your care. May its purpose be fully realized by the power and will of Your grace.

Notes

CHAPTER 1

3   **In the absence of wake-up calls** Covey SR, Merrill AR, Merrill RR. *First Things First.* Simon & Schuster; 1994.

8   **Research shows most people expect joy and fulfillment in their work** Kearney. "Joy at Work." April 1, 2019. https://www.kearney.com/service/leadership-change-organization/article/-/insights/joy-at-work

9   **My first book, Reimagining Workplace Well-Being** Grossmeier J. *Reimagining Workplace Well-Being: Fostering a Culture of Purpose, Connection, and Transcendence.* Modern Wisdom Press; 2022.

CHAPTER 2

17 **What's the point of success** Murthy VH. "My Parting Prescription for America." January 7, 2025. https://www.vivekmurthy.com/partingprescription

20 **Capturing our story in journal prompts** Pennebaker JW, Seagal JD. "Forming a Story: The Health Benefits of Narrative." *Journal of Clinical Psychology.* 1999; 55(1): 1243-1254; Brockington G, Moreira APG, Buso MS, Moll J. Sohal M, Singh P, Dhillon BS, Gill HS. "Efficacy of Journaling in the Management of Mental Illness: A Systematic Review and Meta-analysis." *Family Medicine and Community Health.* 2022; 10(1): e001154.

22 **Harvard Flourishing Index** VanderWeele TJ. "On the Promotion of Human Flourishing." *Proceedings of the National Academy of Sciences.* 2017; 31: 8148-8156. This work is licensed under a Creative Commons Attribution-NonCommercial 4.0 International License.

CHAPTER 3

27 **We are not human beings having a spiritual experience** While this quote is often attributed to the philosopher, priest, and paleontologist Pierre Teilhard de Chardin, there is no verifiable evidence of this quote in his published written works. The quote appears three times in motivational author Wayne W. Dyer's 1989 book, *You'll See it When You Believe It: The Way to Your Personal Transformation.* [William Morrow & Company; 1989] Later works by Stephen Covey attributed the quote to Teilhard de Chardin. Quote Investigator, June 20, 2019. https://quoteinvestigator.com/2019/06/20/spiritual/

28 **in 2019, I edited a special section** Grossmeier J. "Addressing Spiritual Well-being in the Workplace." *American Journal of Health Promotion.* 2019; 33(7): 1081-1093.

29 **growing body of research that supports spirituality as an essential domain of well-being** Long KNG, Symons X, Vanderweele TJ, Balboni TA. "Spirituality As A Determinant of Health: Emerging Policies, Practices, and Systems." *Health Affairs.* 2024; 43(6): 783-790; Puchalski CM, Vitillo R, Hull SK, Reller N. "Improving the Spiritual Dimension of Whole Person Care: Reaching National and International Consensus." *Journal of Palliative Medicine.* 2014; 17(6): 642-656.

31 **The Fetzer Institute has been studying** Fetzer Institute. "Study of Spirituality in the United States." 2020. https://fetzer.org/resources/what-does-spirituality-mean-us

32 **definition for spirituality** American Academy of Family Physicians. "Spirituality and Health." *American Family Physician.* 2001; 63(1): 89. https://www.aafp.org/pubs/afp/issues/2001/0101/p89.html

32 **Others describe spirituality this way** Puchalski C, Ferrell B, Virani R, et al. "Improving the Quality of Spiritual Care as a Dimension of Palliative Care: The Report of the Consensus Conference." *Journal of Palliative Medicine.* 2009; 12(10). https://doi.org/10.1089/jpm.2009.0142

32 **Fetzer's ongoing research found** Fetzer Institute. "What Does Spirituality Mean to Us? A Study of Spirituality in the United States Since COVID." 2023. https://spiritualitystudy.fetzer.org/

33 **National Wellness Institute's 1976 seminal model** National Wellness Institute. "The National Wellness Institute's Six Dimensions of Wellness." 2023. https://nationalwellness.org/resources/six-dimensions-of-wellness/

33 **Ten years after that model was published** Chapman L. "Spiritual Health: A Component Missing from Health Promotion." *American Journal of Health Promotion.* 1986; 1(1): 38-41.

33 **the US Army has been taking a data driven approach** Sellers RF. "Spiritual Readiness." NCO Journal. August 30, 2024; https://www.armyupress.army.mil/Journals/NCO-Journal/Archives/2024/August/Spiritual-Readiness/

33 **Researchers at Gallup have identified five factors of spirituality** Gallup. "Faith and Wellness: The Worldwide Connection Between Spirituality and Wellbeing." 2023. https://www.faithandmedia.com/research/gallup

33 **some organizations are recognized as being faith friendly** Religious Freedom & Business Foundation. "Benchmarking Faith-Friendly Workplaces." 2025. https://religiousfreedomandbusiness.org/redi

33 **researchers from McKinsey Health Institute** Coe E and Enomoto K. "In Search of Self and Something Bigger: A Spiritual Health Exploration." McKinsey Health Institute. May 2024. https://www.mckinsey.com/mhi/our-insights/in-search-of-self-and-something-bigger-a-spiritual-health-exploration

34 **university settings have long included spirituality** Grossmeier J. "Why It's Time to Address Spirituality as Part of a Comprehensive Approach to Workplace Well-being." *American Journal of Health Promotion.* 2025; 39(2): 348-365.

CHAPTER 4

37 **It's not how much money we make** Gladwell M. *Outliers: The Story of Success.* Little, Brown, and Company; 2008.

41 **top drivers of thriving identified by researchers at Mercer** Mercer. "Global Talent Trends 2024: Workforce 2.0." 2024. https://www.mercer.com/assets/global/en/shared-assets/local/attachments/pdf-2024-global-talent-trends-report-en.pdf

42 **Gallup researchers started measuring** Pendell R. "U.S. Employee Life Evaluation Hits New Record Low." Gallup. November 18, 2024. https://www.gallup.com/workplace/653396/employee-life-evaluation-hits-new-record-low.aspx

42 **executive leaders naming employee well-being** Business Group on Health. "15th Annual Employer-Sponsored Health and Well-being Survey: Employers' Steadfast Commitment to Employee Well-being." May 29, 2024. https://www.businessgrouphealth.org/en/Resources/15th-annual-health-and-well-being-survey-2024

42 **Gartner research indicates 82% of employees** Gartner. "6 Predictions for the Future of Performance Management." October 14, 2021. https://www.gartner.com/en/articles/6-predictions-for-the-future-of-performance-management

42 **about half of all employees find their jobs fulfilling** Horowitz JM, Parker K. "How Americans View Their Jobs." Pew Research Center. March 30, 2023. https://www.pewresearch.org/social-trends/2023/03/30/how-americans-view-their-jobs

42 **Work can be defined as a meaningful expression** Martela F, Pessi AB. "Significant Work Is About Self-Realization and Broader Purpose: Defining the Key Dimensions of Meaningful Work." *Frontiers in Psychology.* 2018; 9: 363. https://pmc.ncbi.nlm.nih.gov/articles/PMC5879150/pdf/fpsyg-09-00363.pdf

43 **to be seen as complex human beings with rich, full lives** Gartner. "Employees Seek Personal Value and Purpose at Work. Be Prepared to Deliver. March 29, 2003. https://www.gartner.com/en/articles/employees-seek-personal-value-and-purpose-at-work-be-prepared-to-deliver

43 **Journalist Adam Chandler argues in his book** Chandler A. *99% Perspiration: A New Working History of the American Way of Life.* Penguin Random House; 2025.

43 **According to research by the Society of Human Resource Management** SHRM. "The Importance of Civility in the U.S." 2025. https://www.shrm.org/topics-tools/topics/civility

44 **One 2024 global survey estimates 81% of workers** Hayes J. "81% of the Workforce Is at Risk for Burnout." April 29, 2024. https://www.forbes.com/sites/julianhayesii/2024/04/29/82-of-the-workforce-is-at-risk-for-burnout-heres-what-ceos-can-d0/

44 **See my 2022 book for more information** Grossmeier J. *Reimagining Workplace Well-being: Fostering a Culture of Purpose, Connection, and Transcendence.* Modern Wisdom Press; 2022.

CHAPTER 5

51 **If one does not know to which port** Seneca. *Moral Letters to Lucilius.* Letter 71, section 3. Translated by Richard M. Gummere. Available from https://libquotes.com/seneca/quote/lbt5f6w

57 **Dr. Victor J. Strecher's book** Strecher VJ. *Life on Purpose: How Living for What Matters Most Changes Everything.* HarperCollins; 2016.

60 **you don't need a grand purpose statement for your life** AshaRani PV, Lai D, Koh JX, Subramaniam M. "Purpose in Life in Older Adults: A Systematic

Review on Conceptualization, Measures, and Determinants." *International Journal of Environmental Research and Public Health.* 2022; 19: 5860. https://pmc.ncbi.nlm.nih.gov/articles/PMC9141815/pdf/ijerph-19-05860.pdf

60 **Ego-oriented goals** Kaplan A, Flum H. "Achievement Goal Orientations and Identity Formation Styles." *Educational Research Review.* 2010; 5(1): 50-67.

CHAPTER 6

65 **Connection is the energy that is created** Brown B. *The Gifts of Imperfection: Let Go of Who You Think You're Supposed to Be and Embrace Who You Are.* Hazelden Publishing; 2010.

69 **one in three say they feel lonely at least once a week** American Psychiatric Association. "New APA Poll: One in Three Americans Feels Lonely Every Week." January 20, 2024. https://www.psychiatry.org/News-room/News-Releases/New-APA-Poll-One-in-Three-Americans-Feels-Lonely-E

69 **persona archetypes for extraverts and introverts** Jung CG, Baynes HG. *Psychologische Typen.* Rascher; 1921; Psychologist World. "Extraversion and Introversion." 2025. https://www.psychologistworld.com/influence-personality/extraversion-introversion#references

70 **social connection is as important as quitting smoking** Holt-Lunstad JB, Smith TB, Layton JBB. "Social Relationships and Mortality Risk: A Meta-Analytic Review." *PLOS Medicine.* 2010; 72(6): 517-530.

70 **we tend to take better care of ourselves when we feel cared for** Taylor SE. "Social Support: A Review." In: H. S. Friedman (Ed.). *The Oxford Handbook of Health Psychology* (pp. 189-214). Oxford University Press; 2011; Gallagher S, Rice A, Tierney S, et al. "Social Support and Self-Care in Heart Failure." *Journal of Cardiovascular Nursing.* 2011; 26(6): 439-445.

70 **Higher levels of social support are linked** Mersha AG, Eftekhari P, Bovill M, et al. "Predictors of Adherence to Smoking Cessation Medications Among Current and Ex-smokers in Australia. *International Journal of Environmental Research and Public Health*. 2021; 18(22), 12225; de Dios MA, Stanton CA, Cano MA, et al. "The Influence of Social Support on Smoking Cessation Treatment Adherence Among HIV+ Smokers." *Nicotine & Tobacco Research*. 2016; 18(5), 1126-1133; Salinas J, O'Donnell A, Kokis DJ, et al. "Association of Social Support with Brain Volume and Cognition." *JAMA Network Open*. 2021; 4(8), e2121122; Lee Y, Chi I, Palinkas LA. "Distinct Functions of Social Support and Cognitive Function Among Older Adults." *The Gerontologist*. 2019; 59(4), 384-393; Hsu TW, Ryherd K, Hung TW, et al. "A Neural Signature of Social Support Mitigates Negative Emotion." *Scientific Reports*. 2023; 13, 16263; Gariépy G, Honkaniemi H, Quesnel-Vallée A. "Social Support and Protection from Depression: Systematic Review of Current Findings in Western Countries." *The British Journal of Psychiatry*. 2016; 209(4), 284-293; Harandi T.F, Taghinasab MM, Nayeri TD. "The Correlation of Social Support with Mental Health: A Meta-analysis." *Electronic Physician*. 2017; 9(9), 5212-5222; Seethamraju S, Bhattacharya J, Srinivasan P. "A Systematic Review and Meta-analysis of the Association Between Physical Capability, Social Support, Loneliness, Depression, Anxiety, and Life Satisfaction in Older Adults." *The Gerontologist*. 2024; 64(11), gnae128.

70 **study of employees working in a long-term care setting** Barsade SG, O'Neill OA. "What's Love Got to Do with It? A Longitudinal Study of the Culture of Companionate Love and Employee and Client Outcomes in a Long-Term Care Setting." *Administrative Science Quarterly*. 2014; 59(4): 551-598.

70 **Social support at work has a buffering effect** Cohen S, Wills TA. "Stress Social Support and the Buffering Hypothesis." *Psychological Bulletin*. 1985; 98(2): 310-357.

70 **Evidence links chronic loneliness** Qiao L, Wang G, Tang Z, et al. "Association Between Loneliness and Dementia Risk: A Systematic Review and Meta-Analysis of Cohort Studies." *Frontiers in Human Neuroscience.* 2022; 16, 899814; Luchetti M, Aschwanden D, Sesker AA, et al. "A Meta-Analysis of Loneliness and Risk of Dementia Using Longitudinal Data from >600,000 Individuals." *Nature Mental Health.* 2024; 2: 1350-1361; Valtora NK, Kanaan M, Gilbody S, et al. "Loneliness and Social Isolation as Risk Factors for Coronary Heart Disease and Stroke: Systematic Review and Meta-Analysis of Longitudinal Observational studies." *Heart.* 2016; 102(13), 1009-1016; Smith KJ, Gavey S, Riddell NE, et al. "The Association Between Loneliness, Social Isolation and Inflammation: A Systematic Review and Meta-Analysis." *Neuroscience & Biobehavioral Reviews.* 2020; 112, 519-541; Wang F, Gao Y, Zhen H, et al. "A Systematic Review and Meta-Analysis of 90 Cohort Studies of Social Isolation, Loneliness, and Mortality." *Nature Human Behaviour.* 2023; 7, 1307-1319.

70 **One published review found** Spithoven AWM, Bijttebier P, Goossens L. "It Is All in Their Mind: A Review on Information Processing Bias in Lonely Individuals. *Clinical Psychology Review.* 2017; 58, 97-114.

70 **According to a Harvard Business Review article** Hadley CN, Wright SL. "We're Still Lonely at Work." *Harvard Business Review.* November-December, 2024. https://hbr.org/2024/11/were-still-lonely-at-work

71 **Holt-Lunstad identifies three major types** Holt-Lunstad J. "Why Social Relationships Are Important for Physical Health: A Systems Approach to Understanding and Modifying Risk and Protection." *Annual Review of Psychology.* 2018; 69: 437-458.

74 **U.S. Surgeon General released an advisory** Office of the Surgeon General. "Our Epidemic of Loneliness and Isolation: The US Surgeon General's Advisory on the Healing Effects of Social Connection and Community." Health and Human Services. Published May 2023. https://www.hhs.gov/sites/default/files/surgeon-general-social-connection-advisory.pdf

74 **Gallup researchers report that in 2024** Pendell R. "1 in 5 Employees Worldwide Feel Lonely." Gallup Workplace. June 12, 2024. https://www.gallup.com/workplace/645566/employees-worldwide-feel-lonely.aspx

74 **another 2024 study found that in-person** Hadley CN, Wright SL. "We're Still Lonely at Work." *Harvard Business Review.* November-December, 2024. https://hbr.org/2024/11/were-still-lonely-at-work

74 **Dr. Jim Loehr distinguishes between** Loehr J, Kenney C. *Leading with Character: 10 Minutes a Day to a Brilliant Legacy.* Wiley; 2020.

80 **University of Michigan Center for Positive Organizations** Dutton J, Worline M. "Four Ways to Create High Quality Connections at Work." *Greater Good Magazine.* October 24, 2023. https://greatergood.berkeley.edu/article/item/four_ways_to_create_high_quality_connections_at_work

82 **having a phone out and present** Seppala E. "What Is Your Phone Doing to Your Relationships?" *Greater Good Magazine.* October 10, 2017. https://greatergood.berkeley.edu/article/item/what_is_your_phone_doing_to_your_relationships

CHAPTER 7

93 **We may spend most of our waking hours** Haidt J. *The Righteous Mind: Why Good People Are Divided by Politics and Religion.* Vintage Books; 2012.

96 **Research shows most of us have experienced it.** Kaufman SB. *Transcend: The New Science of Self-Actualization.* Penguin Random House; 2020.

97 **Research on transcendence focuses** Yaden DB, Haidt J, Hood RW, et al. "The Varieties of Self-Transcendent Experience." *Review of General Psychology.* 2017; 21(2): 143-160.

97 **this blurring of separation results** d'Aquili E, Newberg AB. *The Mystical Mind: Probing the Biology of Religious Experience.* Fortress Press; 1999.

98 **Researchers have been able to stimulate** Kaufman SB. *Transcend: The New Science of Self-Actualization.* Penguin Random House; 2020.

98 **Most of the research on the benefits** For a detailed discussion about the benefits of transcendent mental states and original research studies, see chapter 6 of Grossmeier J. *Reimagining Workplace Well-being: Fostering a Culture of Purpose, Connection, and Transcendence.* Modern Wisdom Press; 2022. See also Kaufman SB. *Transcend: The New Science of Self-Actualization.* Penguin Random House; 2020.

99 **We tend to be more open-minded** Goleman D, Davidson RJ. *Altered Traits: Science Reveals How Meditation Changes Your Mind, Brain, and Body.* Avery; 2017.

99 **experiencing awe expands our perception** Rudd M, Vohs KD, Aaker J. "Awe Expands People's Perception of Time, Alters Decision Making, and Enhances Well-being." *Psychological Science.* 2012; 23(10): 1130-1136.

99 **This increases our ability to respond** Piff PK, Dietze P, Feinberg M, et al. "Awe, the Small Self, and Prosocial Behavior." *Journal of Personality and Social Psychology.* 2015; 108(6): 883-899.

100 **Transcendence can be experienced by individuals** Kaufman SB. *Transcend: The New Science of Self-Actualization.* Penguin Random House; 2020.

100 **describes the practice of prayer** ter Kuile C. *The Power of Ritual: Turning Everyday Activities Into Soulful Practices.* HarperCollins; 2020.

103 **Experiencing nature is one of the most** Keltner D. *Awe: The New Science of Wonder and How It Can Transform Your Life.* Penguin Books; 2023.

106 **A 2014 study found** Wilson TD, Reinhard DA, Westgate EC, et al. "Just Think: The Challenges of the Disengaged Mind." *Science.* 2014; 345(6192): 75-77.

107 **Some estimates say we are interrupted** Wulfhorst E. "U.S. Worker Interruptions Costly, Research Shows." August 9, 2007. https://www.reuters.com/article/technology/us-worker-interruptions-costly-research-shows-idUSN13452627/

108 **A 2017 survey of US white-collar workers** Kachan D, Olano H, Tannenbaum SL, et al. "Prevalence of Mindfulness Practices in the US Workforce: National Health Interview Survey." *Preventing Chronic Disease.* 2017; 14(1): 160034.

108 **Awe walks are a growing interest** Reynolds G. "An 'Awe Walk' Might Do Wonders for Your Well-being." *The New York Times.* October 1, 2020. https://www.nytimes.com/2020/09/30/well/move/an-awe-walk-might-do-wonders-for-your-well-being.html

111 **research on volunteerism notes** Nichol B, Wilson R, Rodrigues A, Haighton C. "Exploring the Effects of Volunteering on the Social, Mental, and Physical Health and Well-being of Volunteers: An Umbrella Review." *Voluntas.* May 4, 2023. https://pmc.ncbi.nlm.nih.gov/articles/PMC10159229/pdf/11266_2023_Article_573.pdf

CHAPTER 8

115 **Not only do we understand** Vogl C. *Storytelling for Leadership: Creating Authentic Connections.* Apocryphile Press; 2020.

121 **Habits are individual practices** Duhigg C. *The Power of Habit: Why We Do What We Do in Life and Business.* Random House; 2012.

121 **Rituals are a sequence of practices** This definition is an amalgamation of several sources including ter Kuile C. *The Power of Ritual: Turning Everyday Activities Into Soulful Practices.* HarperCollins; 2020; Norton M. *The Ritual Effect: From Habit to Ritual, Harness the Surprising Power of Everyday Actions.* Scribner; 2024; Ozenc K, Hagan M. *Rituals for Work.* John Wiley & Sons; 2019.

122 **the benefits of cultivating** Norton M. *The Ritual Effect: From Habit to Ritual, Harness the Surprising Power of Everyday Actions.* Scribner; 2024.

123 **Recipe for creating replenishing routines** Norton M. *The Ritual Effect: From Habit to Ritual, Harness the Surprising Power of Everyday Actions.* Scribner; 2024; Ozenc K, Hagan M. *Rituals for Work.* John Wiley & Sons; 2019.